Under the
Golden Pagoda

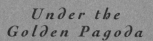

THE BEST OF

BURMESE
COOKING

AUNG AUNG TAIK

design
and illustrations by
CLARE KOSSMAN

CHRONICLE BOOKS
SAN FRANCISCO

dedicated to my mother, Daw Nu Nu Htin,
and my dear friend Roberta Scott

and special thanks to MuMu DeLong,
George Scrivani, Neeli Cherkovski,
Kelly Tuten, Deborah Roberts

Library of Congress
Cataloging-in-Publication Data

Taik, Aung Aung, 1948 -
Under the Golden Pagoda: The Best of
Burma's Cuisine/by Aung Aung Taik;
Design and Illustrations by Clare Kossman
p.cm.
Includes index.
ISBN 0-87701-833-2 (pb)
1. Cookery. Burmese. I. Title
TX724.5.B93T35 1993
641.59591-dc20

92-18405
CIP

Printed in the United States.

Distributed in Canada by Raincoast Books,
112 East Third Ave., Vancouver, B.C. V5T 1C8

10 9 8 7 6 5 4 3 2 1

Chronicle Books
275 Fifth Street
San Francisco, CA 94103

When I left Burma (since renamed Myanmar) in 1972 and landed in the United States, I was a man who knew only eating. My mother, who had spoiled me with her cooking back in Rangoon (now known as Yangon), warned me that if I wanted to continue eating good Burmese food in this land of multinational individuals, I would have to learn to cook for myself.

Having been brought up in a traditional agricultural society, I found nothing could prepare me for the wide variety of foods available in the great industrial cities of America. It also seemed as if almost every ethnic group in those sprawling metropolises was represented by a restaurant or two. But I soon found that the quality of restaurant cooking varied as much as the cultures themselves, and that there were many restaurants offering a sort of hybrid cuisine—a menu tailored to appeal to what was then the rather timid American palate.

In the eighties, a kind of revolution took place in the way Americans looked at food, their own as well as that of other nationalities. Better restaurants seemed to be shifting more and more toward presenting authentic ethnic dishes. America was learning how to cook. And at the same time, my mother was taking me under her blessed wing and guiding me along the great path of Burmese cuisine that she had inherited.

Learning about my adopted homeland went hand in hand with my mother's tutelage in the art of Burmese cooking. Her enthusiasm for America and for cooking and feeding its people was infectious, and as my apprenticeship continued, I soon found myself taking an active role in her catering business. Back in Burma I had known and come to love her independent spirit, her willingness to strike out in the restaurant business in the face of my father's strong objections. Now I saw her bravery acted out again in the way she doggedly stuck to the traditions of our cuisine, despite the warnings of friends who were fearful of her standards of authenticity or who asked that a dish be toned down in deference to some honored American guest whom they assumed could not bear the full brunt of "real" Burmese cooking. Against this tendency to corrupt or adulterate ethnic cooking, a tendency that I have since learned is at work in all the great cuisines as they are practiced in America, we threw ourselves into the task of introducing Americans to a taste and style of cooking little known outside its native borders.

Educated in Burma as an artist, I found that cooking could play a powerful role in my chosen craft. It is said in Burma that contemplation, whether on the beautiful or on the true, cannot proceed on an empty stomach. With one eye toward the new movement in America for preparing authentic ethnic dishes and the other set firmly on the tradition of Burmese cooking practiced by my mother, I grew into an American not only with a grounding in my native tables, but with something of a talent for interpreting that elusive thing called palate, as it is known in Burma. More and more I found myself not only cooking professionally and for friends, but also recounting stories of my native land and its traditions and instructing interested students in the art of Burmese cooking. It is out of this experience that this book has grown.

B urma abounds with vegetation. Indeed, it seems as if practically anything will grow there. In this arcadia the Burmese live in good-natured contentment. Their thoughts are directed to the essence of amusement and their beliefs concern what is universal. From an economic standpoint, Burma is a poor nation. But looking at the dinner table of a farming family, one might easily forget the impoverishment and succumb to the aromas of a simple meal: a curry made with catfish freshly caught from a nearby stream, stir-fried watercress that grows wild next to the hut, some sliced green mangoes to dip in a tangy fish paste, steamed rice, and a delicate gourd soup to complete the picture. Personal gratification with one's existence comes from the dharma, the Buddhist teaching we receive at an early age that makes us all gentlemen and ladies of leisure when we come to the table.

On a map of Southeast Asia, Burma appears shaped like a peacock standing between two great nations, China on the east and India on the west. Modern historians assert that Burma came about as a nation around the eighth or ninth century A.D., a chronicle that would draw objections from many Burmese. For us, Burma begins at Tagung. It is reckoned that Tagung was founded hundreds of years before the birth of Buddha (563 B.C.) by a king of the Sakya, members of a warrior caste who had migrated from India. It is believed that the capital was reestablished by a second refugee prince around the sixth century B.C. From this venerable legend comes the first mention of food in my native land: While out hunting boar, a royal brother of the king of Tagung came to a beautiful place called Srikshetra (where the present-day city of Prome, about 150 miles north of Rangoon, stands) and settled down there to live the life of a hermit. One day, while walking by the river, he spotted a raft carrying two princes drifting downstream. He later learned they were his nephews, both blinded from birth and cast off by their father. The young men, so the story goes, carried with them a supply of food cooked and prepared in a certain way to last for many months—Burma's original larder. I have spent many a delightful hour wondering what might have been among their provisions.

Although modern historians contend that the Burmese are descended from a line of Mongol people, our traditions, folklores, and cuisines spring more from the nucleus of India than from our neighbor to the north. One can easily verify this after thoroughly examining the nature of Burmese cooking. But it is also important not to disregard the presence of the Mon in the genesis of Burmese cuisine. Much earlier than the eighth century, the Mons, who immigrated from the east in what is now known as Cambodia, were already a power in Burma's great Irrawaddy delta and in the south. They were in a constant struggle with the Burmese for superiority. The conquest of the Mon capital of Thaton in 1057 by the Burmese king Anawratha of Pagan was the first successful integration of Mon culture in Burma. So, in tasting Cambodian cuisine, one might be tempted to say, "Ah, there is something Burmese about it." In addition to the Mons, the Thai Chinese, who arrived later, have also provided us with unique influence that is found throughout the eastern part of the country.

In a land as large as Texas, Burma is home to approximately 125 ethnic groups with distinct cultures of their own. The most important of these groups are the Shans, Karens, Mons, Kachins, Chins, and Arakanese; each has its own state and a degree of political autonomy. Even though Burma on paper is an indivisible union of states, the political aspirations of its various ethnic groups have never been uniform. Each group is always trying to break away from the whole. In 1989, the country's military government attempted to solve this secession problem by changing the name of Burma, which reflects only one ethnic group, to Myanmar, which stands for all of the many ethnicities living within the nation's boundaries. Whether this new name will stick depends on political developments that are still in the making. But the links that tie together the country's many ethnic groups must be viewed as the same bridges upon which the inspiration for Burmese cuisine is built.

When the Burmese deposed King Thibaw in 1885 and thereby brought an end to Burmese royalty, the country became a haven for trade and a destination for many foreigners, mostly Indians and Chinese. These new people brought their native cuisines with them. Today, in the big cities such as Rangoon and Mandalay, Burmese restaurants are far outnumbered by Indian and Chinese ones. And so, the best Burmese cuisine is found in Burmese homes. Certainly there are hundreds of marketplaces, small, simple restaurants, and food stalls that sell Burmese dishes. But if a grand dinner, skillfully and elaborately prepared, is what is called for, then a Burmese home is the place to find it.

Burmese do love to go to restaurants serving Indian or Chinese food, however. These two groups offer quite a few choices from which to pick including Indian Muslim or Hindu fare; the food of the Chettyars, a caste of south Indian merchants; the dishes of the minority Panthay, a Muslim-Chinese mix; and a great variety of Chinese cuisines, among which Yunnan and Hakka are particular favorites. Because of this multicultural culinary landscape, a Burmese is likely to want to eat a meal that combines Indian samosas, a Burmese noodle salad or some Chinese egg foo yung, a very un-Chinese coconut rice, a south Indian mulligatawny soup, and a Burmese shrimp curry with fresh cilantro. Such diversity would not seem incompatible to him. Faced with variety, the Burmese will let his or her taste buds decide what complements what.

But what is true Burmese cooking? The simplest way to answer that question is to take an informal approach and say that Burmese food is everything that is commonly cooked and eaten in Burma except for Chinese, Thai, and Indian dishes. That said, a full knowledge of Burmese cuisine must still always include "a tip of the hat" to the contributions of the tables of China, Thailand, and India.

In Burma, a life in harmony with the environment depends upon the family. It is not uncommon for three and sometimes four generations to live in the same house. Because of this custom of togetherness, cooking becomes a collective effort, with each member of the household lending a helping hand.

The typical Burmese kitchen is simple and without modern appliances. Approximately 2 percent of the population uses electricity in the kitchen; the remaining households fuel their cooking with kerosene or charcoal. The country's average year-round temperature is 95° F, so most people never see ice, and refrigeration plays little or no role in daily cooking. Everything is caught or purchased and prepared the day it is eaten. In fact, a deep frying pan with slanted sides and a few pots for making soups, curries, and the like are all that are needed for preparing Burmese food.

Getting up early and heading to the local marketplace is always a delight. The noises and sights of these commercial strongholds are colorful: sellers hawking their goods and buyers making bargains, dhoti-clad coolies running back and forth asking for work, trishaw drivers ringing their bells to attract riders. Faces are familiar among shoppers and sellers, and there is always a good chance of meeting a friend and having a short chat. At times, if my mother bought goods from a different seller instead of at her regular stall, the grocer would gripe and scold her, in a loving way. Occasionally, a fight between shopkeepers would break out in which each would accuse the other of stealing customers.

After an hour or so of shopping, it is time for a breakfast treat, and the market's many food stalls each offer a specialty. Customers are tempted by *mohingar* (fish soup), *ohnokaukswe* (coconut noodle soup), *kaungnyin paung* (glutinous rice with black-eyed peas), and *nanpyar* (flat bread).

Once back home with the morning's purchases, the kitchen suddenly livens. Someone lights the fire, and the others clean and cut the meat or fish, or peel the onions, garlic, and ginger and grind them in a stone mortar. The preparation of a meal is always accompanied by friendly chatter, laughing, teasing, and joking among family members.

Of all our worldly possessions, food is the one thing that a Burmese must share unconditionally and ungrudgingly. A stranger will offer half his banana if you happen to meet his eyes while he is peeling it. When visiting friends and relatives, the first thing that is said, even before "How are you," is "Have you eaten?" Next, it is insisted that you join the family if they are about to eat. And if they have already eaten and you have not, they will go out of their way to prepare you a meal. At times, out of shyness, someone might fib and say that he or she has already eaten. But the host knows how to read a hungry face. Most of my friends were not well-to-do, but when I visited their homes, there would be an invitation to join them in their simple meals—a bowl of hot steamed rice mixed with a little peanut oil and salt and a small piece of dried fish as a token of relative prosperity. I remember enjoying that unadorned fare as much as those lavish dishes cooked in my own family's kitchen.

Whenever a modest meal is offered in genuine hospitality, one must honor it. The monks, on their rounds asking for alms, will stop at any house regardless of its status. They approach your front door and then ring a bell to let you know of their presence. With their eyes closed, they open the cover of their begging bowls and accept whatever is offered. A spoonful of rice is merit enough.

When I was in Burma, I traveled extensively in the districts, trying to capture their lush, beautiful landscapes on canvas. Even though there were no hotels, I was always assured a place to rest and freshen myself by the courtesy of villagers. And being grateful for the hospitality, I would contribute the expense of the nightly meals we ate together. A villager is remarkably humble by nature, but when it comes to cooking, nothing is spared. And if the village has a monastery, an artist can always flatter his way to dinner with the chief monk by offering to paint his portrait, an offer he would not refuse. The style of cooking in the monastery kitchen is a thing unto itself, since the *kapiya*, or monastic chef, must invent and improvise dishes from what is donated. Monks never shop for food. Occasionally my mother would tell our cook to prepare a monastery-style meal, which meant not shopping that day and cooking whatever there was in and around the house. I have been to the most remote parts of Burma, and, to my surprise, I always found a monastery that was able to provide me with good food.

Life in the districts is sweet, and the regional dishes are a delight and highly prized. It is customary for Burmese to bring back some unique or renowned preparation from a province as a gift upon returning home, since these specialists are seldom found elsewhere. Sweet rice dishes from Moulmein; sour shrimp pâtés, crab sauce, and fish chutneys from Pyapon and Bassein; preserved meats from Meikhtila; seafood delights from Mergui, to name a few. Nobody comes empty-handed as a visitor, nor returns empty-handed from a trip.

The twelve months of the Burmese lunar calendar are marked with major festivals, and all the festivals are celebrated with special foods. In addition to these important events, there are endless festivals that can be found on almost any day of the year at the country's many pagoda grounds, from Rangoon's great Shwedagon to the little-known pagoda at Ohnare village. The festivities bring dance troupes, skits, magic shows, boxing matches, curio shops, and the ubiquitous food stalls selling seasonal dishes. *Htamane*, a thick stew of glutinous rice mixed with sesame seeds, peanuts, ginger, coconut, and oil, is made in the month of Tabodwe (approximately February) to celebrate the rice harvest. The year opens with the Shinpyu ceremony, during which young boys of seven years or more enter the monastery for a brief time to devote themselves to prayer. At the same time the young girls participate in a formal ear-piercing ceremony. The foods served at a Shinpyu ceremony vary, depending upon whether the celebrants are from a wealthy family or more humble origins. The former will enjoy a meal that consists of as many as four meat and four fish and shellfish dishes, plus a vegetable, soup, and rice. A middle-class family will sit down to fewer dishes or may simply order *biryani* (a meat-and-rice dish) from the Indian caterers. For the lower middle class, it is a cake and ice cream affair. And the poor honor the day with a meal of rice, pickled mango, pea curry, and salted fish sautéed with garlic and onions. In April, various snacks made from tapioca are prepared for Thingyan, the Burmese New Year Water-Throwing Festival.

Of course, all year long there are weddings, anniversaries, graduations, births, and, naturally, funerals. Regardless of the occasion there is always a place for food. My wealthy friend Ko Kyaw Gyee of Mandalay is an excellent example of the phrase "always looking for an excuse to celebrate." One day, out of the blue, he came to pick me up, his jeep already loaded with friends, and drove to the best restaurant in town. When we asked him what this was all about, he answered, "Well, around three o'clock this afternoon, I heard my father-in-law coughing ominously."

To be in harmony with whatever occurs, Burmese Buddhists hold to the concept of abhidharmma: a commitment to correct the incorrect and to work ceaselessly to attain a fuller understanding of the Buddha's teachings. Being homo sapiens, we find that goal often escapes our consciousness, either because of absentmindedness or because of being too preoccupied with the workaday world. Yet, one thing in life is indispensable, as a famous Burmese saying points out: "One cannot meditate on an empty stomach." Such thinking underlies the importance of eating and food, even in light of perfection. Lord Buddha had to comply with this truth at one point in his life. He saw that going around asking for alms was distracting him from his practice of meditation, so he committed himself to the severe procedure known as dukkhasriya, which entailed eating only fruit that fell in front of him, a path the common man would find impossible to follow. After a while, the Buddha's energy collapsed, as his body shrank to mere skin and bones. With this, he came to realize that extremeness also hindered achieving enlightenment. So, he adopted the famous middle way, which was to resume eating, but to eat moderately.

In an agricultural society, one doesn't usually burden one's self with thoughts of whether air is more important than food for survival. Or even where, when, or how the universe came about. After we have fulfilled our day's servitude, we eat and enjoy ourselves at the table, savoring the food cooked in the tradition of our land. The rising steam from the dishes fans our smiles. Only after this grateful meal can we lie peacefully on a bamboo mat, puff away on a cheroot, and think about building the stupa of merit.

Rice is the backbone of Burmese cuisine, the centerpiece of every meal. With the rice, the Burmese eat meat in moderation and vegetables, making for a well-balanced, healthful diet.

I have recommended complementary accompaniments for some recipes, but I would like to exhort readers to use their own judgment on assembling a meal, since all the recipes in this book are highly complementary and are pleasing to the Western palate. My serving portions are very generous, for a Burmese never wants to see every morsel on the table eaten. Such a situation would mean that he or she was a bad host because not enough food was served.

The Burmese are early risers. They believe that to observe the sun rising has merit in itself. By dawn, people are up and about preparing offerings for the monks, going to the market, or taking walks and doing exercises. Breakfast is often a fish soup, coconut chicken noodles, or a glutinous rice dish, bought at the marketplace or from vendors who come to the neighborhood.

Home-cooked lunches and dinners are usually one meat or seafood dish along with vegetables, soup, and plain rice. Almost all Burmese eat with their fingers: the right hand takes the place of both knife and fork, and the left is used for serving dishes that are set in the middle of the table and shared. If there are foreign guests present, the Burmese will frequently compromise and eat with a fork and spoon. Knives are rarely used.

Soup is served in individual bowls with spoons at most cosmopolitan homes. In the rural districts, soup is served in a common bowl. Both soup and salad are served with the main dishes, not as separate courses. Appetizers and desserts are reserved for when guests are present or for ceremonial occasions. Otherwise the final course is tea without milk or sugar and fresh fruit of the season. A short stroll after the meal is a common practice.

The following are broad guidelines for serving a Burmese meal:

For Simple Family Meals meat, poultry, or seafood dish; vegetable; soup; steamed rice; and tea.

For Informal Meals appetizers, poultry, meat, fish or shellfish, salad, vegetable, soup, steamed rice, fresh fruit, and tea or coffee.

For Formal Meals appetizers, chicken, beef, pork, fish, shellfish, salad, vegetable, soup, fancy rice dish, homemade dessert, and tea or coffee.

The dishes in this chapter are generally eaten in Burma as snacks and only occasionally as part of a meal. Just as the French always have time for their wine, the Burmese are crazy for snacks. I personally think that they eat snacks less from appetite than out of a kind of gastronomic lust.

An endless variety of snacks are sold at food stalls or by vendors who howl their delights as they walk. I remember afternoons in Rangoon when my friends and I would summon the sellers one after the other, even though we had just enjoyed a hearty lunch.

Except for those who are westernized, Burmese do not host cocktail receptions where appetizers are passed amongst the guests. It is considered improper to have guests drink and eat while standing. At any given ceremony, we are obliged to be served while sitting on chairs or on mats on the ground.

In other words, I have called these delicacies appetizers only because in America I find them very suitable for that purpose.

Butheekyaw

Golden Brown Gourd Strip

One of my favorite late-afternoon dishes that can be purchased at any snack hut in Rangoon. These shops are usually simple thatched structures where the cooking is done, and just outside are low, round tables and bamboo mats where the customers sit and gossip while they eat.

Garlic and Vinegar Sauce (following recipe)
2 pounds bottleneck gourd
2 ripe bananas, peeled and mashed
2 cups rice flour
1 cup glutinous rice flour
1 teaspoon salt
1 teaspoon baking soda
2 cups water
Vegetable oil for frying

Prepare the sauce and set aside.

Peel the gourd. Cut in half lengthwise and scrape out and discard the seeds and pith. Cut the halves into 3-inch-long sections. Slice each section lengthwise into 1/2-inch-thick strips. Place the gourd strips in a large bowl and add the bananas, rice flours, salt, and baking soda; mix well. Slowly add the water, mixing it in with your hands until the mixture is quite pasty.

In a deep frying pan, pour in the oil to a depth of 1 1/2 inches and heat until very hot. Reduce the heat to medium. Take 3 strips, place them next to each other to form a unit, and slip them together into the oil. Repeat with the remaining gourd strips; do not crowd the pan. Fry, turning once, until golden brown on both sides, about 8 minutes per side. Remove with a slotted utensil and drain briefly on paper towels. Repeat with the remaining gourd strips.

Eat immediately accompanied with the dipping sauce.

Serves 4.

Chinnsogar
Garlic and Vinegar Sauce

This sauce is a popular one that is not only served with fried gourd strips, but with Onion Fritters (page 22) and Shrimp Patties (page 26) as well.

8 cloves garlic, finely chopped
1/4 cup dried shrimp powder
1/4 cup distilled white vinegar
1/2 cup fish sauce
1/2 cup fresh lemon juice
1/4 teaspoon crushed red chile pepper, or to taste

Combine all of the ingredients in a bowl. Stir thoroughly and let stand for 30 minutes before serving.

Makes about 1 1/2 cups.

Never underestimate the amount of this dish you will need. A true crowd pleaser, it is the Burmese answer to American onion rings.

Garlic and Vinegar Sauce (page 21)
6 medium-sized yellow onions
1 1/2 cups all-purpose flour
1/2 cup cornstarch
1/2 teaspoon baking powder
1 1/2 cups water
Vegetable oil for frying

Prepare the sauce and set aside.

Cut the onions in half vertically and then slice the halves thinly to form crescent-shaped fans. Put the onion pieces in a large bowl and mix gently with your fingers to break them into individual strips. Add the flour, cornstarch, and baking powder. Slowly add the water, mixing it in with your hands until the mixture is quite pasty.

In a deep frying pan, pour in the oil to a depth of 1 1/2 inches and heat until very hot. Reduce the heat to medium. Form the battered onions into patties about 2 inches in diameter and slip them into the oil; do not crowd the pan. Fry the patties, turning them from time to time, until they are golden brown on both sides, about 8 minutes' total cooking time. Remove with a slotted utensil to paper towels to drain briefly. Repeat with the remaining patties.

Eat immediately accompanied with the sauce.

Serves 4 to 6.

Peiyarkyaw
Split Pea Fritters

In Burma everyone usually buys this snack from an Indian vendor who walks about the neighborhood carrying a small charcoal stove in one hand and the rest of his culinary necessities neatly packed and slung over his shoulders. He will prepare this dish right at the front door.

3 cups yellow split peas
1 large, yellow onion, finely diced
1/2 cup minced fresh cilantro
1 fresh jalapeño pepper, or to taste, chopped
1/2 teaspoon salt
Vegetable oil for frying
1 lemon

Rinse the split peas in cold water; drain. Place the peas in a bowl, add water to cover, and let soak overnight.

Drain the peas and purée them in a food processor or blender. Transfer to a bowl and add the onions, cilantro, pepper, and salt. Using your hands, mix well and form into little balls or patties.

In a deep frying pan, pour in the oil to a depth of 1 1/2 inches and heat until very hot. Reduce the heat to medium. Slip the fritters into the oil; do not crowd the pan. Fry, turning once, until golden brown on both sides, about 5 minutes per side. Remove with a slotted utensil to paper towels to drain briefly. Repeat with the remaining fritters.

Squeeze lemon juice over the fritters just before serving.

Serves 4 to 6.

Khayanthee Paung
Steamed Eggplant

For this recipe you must use the lavender Chinese eggplant, which is firm, long, and slender. Japanese eggplants are softer, stubbier, and darker in color, and will not hold up as well to steaming.

4 cloves garlic, finely minced
1 fresh jalapeño pepper, chopped
1 green onion, chopped
1/4 cup light soy sauce
3 tablespoons Asian sesame oil
Six 8-inch-long Chinese eggplants

In a small bowl, combine the garlic, jalapeño, green onion, soy sauce, and sesame oil. Stir together thoroughly and let stand for 30 minutes.

Meanwhile, pour the water into a steamer pan and bring to a boil. Place the eggplants on a rack over the boiling water, cover, and steam until the eggplants are tender when pierced with a knife, about 15 minutes.

Arrange the eggplants alongside one another on a serving platter. Slice crosswise into 1-inch-thick pieces. Spoon the sauce over the eggplant slices and serve.

Serves 4 to 6.

Pazunhlaw

Salted Shrimp

Shrimp meat is much tastier when cooked in its shell. Although a little messy, shrimp prepared this way can be as irresistible as eating peanuts from the shell. We always bring this dish along when traveling in Burma.

> 1 pound shrimp in the shell, with or without heads
> 1 tablespoon oil
> 1 1/2 teaspoons salt

If the shrimp have heads, cut off the eyes and whiskers with scissors. Heat the oil in a frying pan over medium heat. Add the shrimp and salt and cook, turning once, until the shells are slightly charred on both sides, about 4 minutes' total cooking time.

Serves 4.

Pazun Ngabaung Kyaw
Shrimp Patties

Homemade appetizers were compulsory in my family home in Rangoon. My father would turn into a tyrant if the food didn't meet his expectations or if he felt a dish had been served too often. His attitude was a headache for my mother. This dish was always her solution. It never failed to put a smile on his face.

Garlic and Vinegar Sauce (optional; page 21)
1 pound bay shrimp
1 cup all-purpose flour
$3/4$ cup water
$1/2$ teaspoon salt
1 tablespoon cornstarch
Vegetable oil for frying

Prepare the sauce, if using, and set aside.

In a mixing bowl, place the shrimp, flour, water, salt, and cornstarch. With your hands, mix the ingredients together thoroughly.

In a large frying pan over medium heat, pour in oil to a depth of $1/4$ inch. Form the shrimp mixture into patties about 2 inches in diameter and $1/4$ inch thick and slip them into the oil. Do not crowd the pan. Fry, turning once, until lightly browned on both sides, about 2 minutes per side. Repeat with the remaining patties.

Serve hot accompanied with the sauce for dipping.

Serves 4.

Pazungaung Kyaw
Fried Shrimp Heads

I find that most Americans have a phobia about eating the heads of animals. But in Asia, fish heads and shrimp heads are considered delicacies. I can assure you that the taste of this dish will overcome any hesitation you may have about eating it. Buy shrimp with heads (since you can't buy just the heads) and plan another shrimp dish that uses the bodies as part of the meal.

36 shrimp heads
  (from about 1 pound medium shrimp)
$^1/_2$ cup all-purpose flour
$^1/_4$ teaspoon salt
$^1/_4$ teaspoon ground turmeric
$^1/_2$ cup water
Vegetable oil for frying

Pluck the heads from the shrimp bodies. Cut off the eyes and whiskers with scissors. In a bowl, place the heads, flour, salt, turmeric, and water. With your hands, mix the ingredients together thoroughly.

In a large frying pan over medium heat, pour in oil to a depth of $^1/_4$ inch. Add the batter-coated shrimp heads and fry, turning once, until golden brown, about 3 minutes per side.

Serve immediately.

Serves 4.

Ngalay Kyaw
Fried Smelts

Once, while on an art class field trip near the sea, I took my fishing rod along in the hopes of catching something for dinner And with it, I also brought four pounds of smelts for bait. When my friends saw the amount of bait I had, they thought I was being a bit over ambitious—arrogant, to be precise. At the end of the day, not one of us had caught a fish. What my companions didn't realize was that I had brought my frying pan along as well, which was waiting for the smelts. Suddenly there was a special treat for all the beer drinkers.

3 pounds smelts
1 teaspoon ground turmeric
1 teaspoon salt
Vegetable oil for frying

With scissors, cut along the entire length of the underside of each smelt and remove the entrails. Do not cut off the head, fins, or tail.

In a large bowl, place the smelts, salt, and turmeric. With your hands, mix the ingredients thoroughly.

In a large frying pan, pour in oil to a depth of 1 $^1/_2$ inches. Heat over medium-high heat. Add the smelts and fry, turning once, until golden brown, about 5 minutes per side. Do not worry about crowding the frying pan. Let the smelts stick together while they are frying, then separate them later when they are cool enough to handle. Remove the smelts with a slotted utensil to paper towels to drain.

Serve at room temperature.

Serves 6 to 8.

Kyettaungbun Kyaw
Fried Chicken Wings

In Burma chicken wings come with the chicken, and there is always much fuss over who will get them. Americans seem to have more wings than chickens. What an opportunity to fry them plentifully!

> 10 chicken wings
> 1/2 teaspoon ground turmeric
> 1 1/2 teaspoons finely minced fresh ginger
> 1 1/2 teaspoons finely minced garlic
> 1 teaspoon fresh lemon juice
> 1 tablespoon water
> 1/2 cup all-purpose flour
> 1/2 teaspoon salt
> 1 cup vegetable oil

Remove the wing tips. Cut each wing in half at the joint. In a mixing bowl, combine the wings with all the other ingredients except the oil. Mix thoroughly, cover, and refrigerate for 3 hours.

In a large, deep frying pan, heat the oil over high heat. Add the chicken wings and cook until golden brown on both sides, about 12 minutes' total cooking time.

Serves 4 to 6.

Meats arranged on skewers always look intriguing. It's disappointing to see them undone. I find that there is something very satisfying about eating right off the stick.

2 pounds chicken breasts
1 teaspoon ground lemongrass
1 teaspoon crushed garlic
1/2 teaspoon paprika
1/4 teaspoon ground turmeric
1/2 teaspoon salt
1 teaspoon fish sauce
1 teaspoon light soy sauce
1 teaspoon fresh lemon juice
1 tablespoon vegetable oil
1/2 teaspoon salt

Bone and skin the chicken breasts. Cut the meat into 1/4-inch-thick bite-sized pieces. In a mixing bowl, combine the chicken with all the remaining ingredients. With your hands, mix the ingredients together thoroughly. Cover and refrigerate for 3 to 4 hours.

Soak 4 to 6 thin, 8-inch-long bamboo skewers in water to cover for about 3 hours. Prepare a fire in a charcoal grill or preheat a broiler.

Thread the chicken pieces onto the skewers.

Barbecue or broil the skewered chicken for 3 minutes; turn the skewers and cook until done, about 3 minutes longer. Arrange the skewers on a platter and serve.

Serves 6.

Kyethar Tobu
Chicken Cubes

Getting this recipe from my mother was like rubbing together two rocks for oil. Fortunately, I managed to effect the miracle. These morsels will literally melt in your mouth.

4 cups clear chicken stock
1/4 pound peeled shrimp, finely minced
3 green onions, very thinly sliced
1 1/4 cups cornstarch, dissolved in 2 cups water,
    plus cornstarch for dusting
6 eggs, beaten
1 teaspoon ground black pepper
Vegetable oil for frying
Granulated sugar or chile sauce for serving

Bring the chicken stock to a boil in a large saucepan. Turn the heat to low and add the shrimp, green onions, and pepper. Cook for 3 minutes and stir in the cornstarch-water mixture. While continuing to stir, slowly pour in the eggs to form a thick, yet pourable consistency. Remove the pan from the heat and immediately pour the egg mixture into a 2-foot-square tray with 2-inch sides. Cover and refrigerate until cool.

Cut the chilled egg mixture into 1 1/2-inch squares. Lightly dust the squares with cornstarch. Pour the oil into a large skillet to a depth of 1 inch and place over medium heat. Slip the squares into the oil; do not crowd the pan. Cook, turning once, until golden brown on both sides, about 5 minutes per side. Repeat with the remaining squares. Serve hot with the sugar or chile sauce.

Serves 4 to 6.

These tasty morsels are a nice change from more conventional meatballs.

    1 pound ground pork
    1 teaspoon finely chopped fresh ginger
    1 teaspoon finely chopped garlic
    1 tablespoon light soy sauce
    1 teaspoon cornstarch
    $1/4$ teaspoon ground black pepper
    1 cup vegetable oil

In a mixing bowl, place all the ingredients except the oil. With your hands, mix the ingredients together thoroughly. Let stand for 1 hour.

Form the pork mixture into balls 1 inch in diameter. Heat the oil in a large frying pan over medium heat. Add the balls and fry, turning frequently, until lightly browned, about 3 minutes. Serve with toothpicks.

Serves 2 to 4.

Ahmaighin
Barbecued Beef on Skewers

This dish takes me back to the cinema halls of Rangoon. During intermission, the audience would rush outside to the waiting vendors who were selling skewers of barbecued beef. It was a frenzied scene—everybody in a hurry to satisfy themselves without missing the main feature.

> 2 pounds filet mignon
> $1/4$ teaspoon ground turmeric
> 1 tablespoon ground cumin
> 1 teaspoon paprika
> $1/2$ teaspoon salt
> 1 lime

Cut the beef into 1-inch cubes. In a mixing bowl, place the beef, turmeric, cumin, paprika, and salt. With your hands, mix the ingredients together thoroughly. Cover and marinate overnight in the refrigerator.

Soak 6 medium-thick, 8-inch-long bamboo skewers in water to cover for about 3 hours. Prepare a fire in a charcoal grill or preheat a broiler.

Thread the beef cubes onto the skewers. Barbecue or broil the skewered beef for 3 minutes; turn the skewers and cook until done to taste, about 3 minutes longer for medium-rare.

Cut the lime into quarters and rub over the meat. Arrange the skewers on a platter and serve.

Serves 6.

The Burmese do not regard soup as a first course, in the way that it is in the West. It is consumed along with the other dishes of the meal. The exceptions are fish soup (*mohingar*), coconut noodle soup (*ohnokaukswe*), rice soup (*sanbyoke*), and bean thread soup (*kyarzan chet*), all of which are enjoyed as main courses. Soup is sometimes reheated during a meal so that it is good and hot. There is even a Burmese saying that goes, "Eat hot curry, drink hot soup, burn your lips, and remember my dinner."

Every Burmese meal includes a soup—liquid to help the solids slide down. The fast pace of American life makes serving soup with every meal a luxury. At my mother's, I often notice that there is no soup on the table. "You forgot to make the soup or what?" I'll ask her. She answers, "Hey, I have to work, you know. We all can't be artists like you."

Kazunywat Chinye
Water Spinach Soup

Monsoon season runs for six months in Burma. Since this leafy green vegetable grows everywhere as long as there is water, it has kept the Burmese from famine during troubled times. When I lived in Burma, I knew countless impoverished families whose evening meal consisted of this soup and plain rice. I feel a certain humbleness whenever I serve this dish.

Water spinach, which is sometimes called swamp cabbage, waterconvovolus, or hollow stem vegetable in English and ong choy *or* tung choy *in Cantonese, can be found in the spring and early summer in markets that carry Chinese and Southeast Asian food.*

2 pounds water spinach
2 teaspoons vegetable oil
1 yellow onion, chopped
2 cloves garlic, pounded in a mortar
1/4 teaspoon ground turmeric
1/4 cup shrimp powder
2 teaspoons fish sauce
1/2 cup tamarind juice
6 cups water

Pick off the leaves of the spinach and break the tender stem portions into 3-inch-long pieces. Heat the oil in a medium-sized saucepan over medium heat. Add the onion, garlic, and turmeric and sauté over medium heat until the onion is translucent, about 5 minutes. Add the shrimp powder, fish sauce, tamarind juice, and water and bring to a boil. Lower the heat, add the spinach leaves and stems, and simmer gently for 15 minutes.

Serves 4 to 6.

Peiwahlay Hincho
Split Mung Bean Soup

My American friends find this soup an interesting complement to their European-style dinners. I add this dish to a menu whenever I feel the meal needs something liquid to balance a selection of "firm dishes."

1 cup split mung beans
4 cups water
2 cloves garlic, pounded in a mortar
1/2 teaspoon finely minced fresh ginger
8 curry leaves, or 1 bay leaf
1 teaspoon salt
1/4 teaspoon ground black pepper
3 tablespoons vegetable oil
1 yellow onion, chopped
1/4 teaspoon ground turmeric
1 green onion, finely chopped

Rinse the mung beans in cold water, drain. In a medium-sized pan, bring the water to a boil. Lower the heat and add the mung beans, garlic, ginger, curry leaves, salt, and pepper. Simmer gently until the beans are soft and split, about 30 minutes.

Meanwhile, heat the oil in a small frying pan over medium-high heat. Add the yellow onion and turmeric and fry until golden brown, about 10 minutes. Remove from heat and set aside. When the soup is ready, add the fried onion and green onion and stir for 1 minute. Serve very hot.

Serves 4.

Butheehingar
Bottleneck Gourd Soup

This is the favorite soup to accompany meals at every Burmese food stall. It is also considered a universal panacea, a dish that performs magic, much in the same way as the legendary chicken soup.

2 pounds bottleneck gourds
4 cups water
4 cloves garlic, pounded in a mortar
3 tablespoons shrimp powder
1/2 teaspoon ground black pepper
1/2 teaspoon salt

Peel the gourds. Cut them in half lengthwise and scrape out and discard the seeds and pith. Cut the gourds into slices about 1 inch in diameter and 1/4 inch thick.

Bring the water to a boil in a medium-sized saucepan. Add all the remaining ingredients except the gourd slices and simmer uncovered over medium heat for 15 minutes. Add the gourd and cook until tender, about 10 minutes.

Serves 4.

Buthee Kyawchet

Sautéed Bottleneck Gourd Soup

Although this soup is similar to the plainer Bottleneck Gourd Soup (preceding), it has more body because of its different cooking method and more varied ingredients. It's the rich folks' version of a simple soup.

You can substitute 4 cups sliced zucchini (1/4-inch-thick slices) for the bottleneck gourd in this recipe, to make Zucchini Kyawchet. As far as I know, there's no name for zucchini in Burmese. I have to admit that I am not too crazy about zucchini, with the exception of using it for this soup, a recipe that I created in order to avoid being the only guy in America who doesn't like this ubiquitous vegetable.

2 pounds bottleneck gourds
4 teaspoons cooking oil
1 yellow onion, finely chopped
1/4 teaspoon ground turmeric
1/4 teaspoon paprika
4 cloves garlic, pounded in a mortar
3 tablespoons shrimp powder
1/2 teaspoon ground black pepper
1/2 teaspoon salt
4 cups water

Peel the gourds. Cut them in half lengthwise and scrape out the seeds and pith. Cut the gourds into slices about 1 inch in diameter and 1/4 inch thick. Heat the oil in a medium-sized saucepan over medium-low heat. Add the onion and turmeric and sauté until the onion is translucent, about 5 minutes. Add all the remaining ingredients except the water and sauté for 3 minutes. Add the water and raise the heat to high. As soon as the soup boils, lower the heat and simmer gently until the gourd is tender, about 5 minutes.

Serves 4.

Kalapei Hincho
Yellow Split Pea Soup

Yellow split pea soup was something I had three times a week during my eleven years at boarding school. The teachers would say, "It will make you strong as a horse." No doubt the soup was good. I even enjoyed it. But for eleven years? This recipe is definitely the gourmet version of that soup, perfected through the decades. I attribute much of my continuing strength to this staple dish.

2 cups yellow split peas
1/2 cup vegetable oil
1 medium-sized yellow onion, chopped
3 cloves garlic, minced
1/4 teaspoon ground turmeric
6 cups water
1 bay leaf
1 tablespoon ground cumin
1/2 teaspoon ground coriander
1/4 teaspoon ground cardamom
1/2 teaspoon paprika
1 tablespoon black mustard seed
1 teaspoon salt, or to taste
1/4 cup tamarind juice
1 tablespoon ghee or butter

Rinse the split peas in cold water; drain. Place the split peas in a bowl, add water to cover, and soak overnight; drain and set aside.

Heat the oil in a deep, medium-sized frying pan over medium heat. Add the onion, garlic, and turmeric and sauté until the onion is golden brown, about 10 minutes. Remove the mixture from the pan; set aside.

To the same pan, add the water, drained split peas, bay leaf, cumin, coriander, cardamom, paprika, mustard seed, salt, and tamarind juice. Stir well and bring to a simmer over medium heat. Cook until the peas are very soft and begin to form a smooth mass, about 45 minutes.

Add the reserved onion mixture and ghee. Stir well and cook for 5 minutes. Serve very hot.

Serves 4 to 6.

This soup has a clean, tangy quality to balance rich curry dishes.

1/4 cup vegetable oil
1 yellow onion, finely chopped
3 cloves garlic, pounded in a mortar
1 teaspoon fresh ginger slices
1 tablespoon ground cumin
1/4 teaspoon ground turmeric
1/2 teaspoon ground black pepper
2 bay leaves
1 cup tamarind juice
1 tablespoon distilled white vinegar
2 cups clear chicken stock
1/2 teaspoon salt, or to taste
1/2 teaspoon granulated sugar
4 cups water

Heat the oil in a medium-sized saucepan over medium heat. Add the onion, garlic, ginger, cumin, turmeric, pepper, and bay leaves and sauté, stirring frequently, until the onion begins to soften, 3 minutes.

Add the tamarind juice, vinegar, chicken stock, salt, sugar, and water. Cover and let simmer over medium heat for 45 minutes.

Serves 4.

Mounlar Ou Chinye
Daikon Soup

The Burmese often drink the broth of this soup and then eat the daikon with steamed rice and fried smelts or catfish. In rural areas the soup is usually served in a communal bowl in the center of the table and everyone shares the same spoon in a gesture of camaraderie.

On my first experience with such simplicity, I was somewhat concerned about the hygiene of such a practice. I began to feel more at home after observing the first two members of the family inhale the broth while barely touching the spoon to their lips.

$1/4$ cup vegetable oil
1 yellow onion, thinly sliced
$1/4$ teaspoon ground turmeric
1 teaspoon paprika
$1/2$ cup shrimp powder
2 medium-sized tomatoes, cut into quarters
One 1 $1/2$-pound daikon, peeled and cut
   crosswise into $1/4$-inch-thick slices
$3/4$ cup tamarind juice
2 tablespoons fish sauce
$1/4$ teaspoon granulated sugar
$1/4$ teaspoon salt
10 sprigs fresh cilantro
6 cups water

Heat the oil in a large saucepan over medium heat. Add the onion, turmeric, paprika, shrimp powder, and tomatoes and sauté until the tomatoes are soft, 3 to 5 minutes.

Add the daikon, tamarind juice, fish sauce, sugar, salt, cilantro, and water. Bring to a boil, cover, lower the heat, and simmer for 40 minutes.

Serves 4.

Nwarme Hincho
Oxtail Soup

Animal tails always amuse me. They are an amazing example of nonstop action. Maybe that is why it is said that eating them reanimates and invigorates you. Because of the intricate way the meat is embedded in the tail bone, eating it puts your mouth to work.

2 tablespoons vegetable oil
2 pounds oxtail, cut into 1-inch sections
1 yellow onion, chopped
4 bay leaves
1 cinnamon stick
1 stalk celery
1/4 teaspoon ground turmeric
1 teaspoon salt, or to taste
1 tablespoon light soy sauce
2 cups clear beef stock
4 cups water

Heat the oil in a 2-quart saucepan over medium heat, add the oxtails and brown well on all sides. Add all the remaining ingredients and simmer, covered, until the meat is done, 1 to 2 hours.

Serves 4.

Ahmaiou Pyoke
Tripe Soup

Unlike the tripe sold in American markets, which has been cleaned and bleached, the tripe in Burma has not. This same soup made back home has a stronger taste and aroma.

1 1/2 pounds honeycomb tripe, cut into
  pieces 3/4 inch wide and 2 inches long
4 medium-sized slices fresh ginger
1/4 teaspoon ground lemongrass
2 cups clear chicken stock
4 cloves garlic, crushed
1 teaspoon salt, or to taste
1 tablespoon light soy sauce
1 tablespoon fresh lime juice
6 cups water

Fill a large saucepan with water and add the tripe. Bring to a boil and boil for 15 minutes; drain.

Combine the tripe and all the remaining ingredients in the same saucepan. Bring to a boil over high heat, lower the heat, cover, and simmer until the tripe is cooked, about 1 1/2 hours.

Serves 4.

Seikthar Masala Hincho
Lamb Soup with Green Peas

About a mile from my Rangoon boarding school was a bridge that crossed over the railroad tracks. At one end of the span stood a small tin-roofed cafe owned by Tamils who had immigrated from neighboring India. Most of the cafe's customers were workers from a nearby hospital. This soup was the only item on the menu, and it was served with the Indian bread called naan. My friends and I would sneak out of the school compound and head for the cafe whenever the spirit of wanderlust struck. There we would eat this soup and enjoy the company of the Tamil workers. It was a whole new world for a boy my age. After I graduated from school, I sometimes returned to that simple cafe, the only place where I could capture this particular taste and aroma.

1/4 cup vegetable oil
2 pounds bone-in lamb stew meat (2- to 3-inch pieces)
1 medium-sized yellow onion, finely chopped
1/4 teaspoon ground turmeric
2 teaspoons salt, or to taste
1/2 teaspoon ground black pepper
1 tablespoon ground cumin
2 bay leaves
1 3/4 cups clear chicken stock
6 cups water
3 cups shelled green peas (about 3 pounds unshelled), or
   1 package (17 ounces) frozen green peas, thawed
1 cup half-and-half cream

Heat the oil in a large saucepan over medium heat. Add the lamb, onion, and turmeric and sauté until the lamb is browned, about 5 minutes. Add the salt, pepper, cumin, bay leaves, chicken stock, and water. Cover and simmer for 1 1/2 hours, stirring occasionally.

Add the peas and half-and-half and stir well. Cook for 10 minutes longer.

Serves 4.

Beithar Myuswum Hincho
Duck Soup with Extra-Thin Noodles

When you feel like having a light dinner, this soup is appropriate. I recommend buying a Long Island duck, as the Peking variety found at Chinese markets usually has too much fat.

2 cups preserved mustard greens
One 3-pound Long Island duck
7 cups water
1 1/2 cups clear chicken stock
4 cloves garlic, pounded in a mortar
1 yellow onion, finely chopped
1 teaspoon finely chopped fresh ginger
1/4 cup light soy sauce
1 tablespoon fish sauce
1/2 teaspoon ground black pepper
1/2 teaspoon salt
1 teaspoon granulated sugar
4 ounces extra-thin wheat noodles
1 cup thinly sliced green onion

Rinse the mustard greens in cold water, then soak in cold water to cover for 1 hour. Drain well and cut into 1-inch-thick slices; set aside.

Skin the duck and remove any visible fat. Sever the wings and thighs from the duck, then separate the breast from the back. Place the duck pieces in a large saucepan. Add the water, stock, garlic, onion, ginger, soy sauce, fish sauce, pepper, salt, and sugar. Bring to a boil, cover, lower the heat, and simmer for 1 hour, skimming off any foam that forms on the surface. Remove from the heat.

Remove the duck pieces from the pan, let them cool, and then bone them. Skim off the fat that forms on the surface of the cooled soup. Fifteen minutes before continuing to cook the soup, soak the noodles in cold water to cover; drain.

Return the soup to medium heat and add the duck meat, mustard greens, and noodles. Cover and simmer over medium heat for 15 minutes. Serve garnished with green onion.   Serves 4 to 6.

Sanbyoke
Chicken-Rice Soup

I like to serve this soup at late-night gatherings or after an evening's entertainment. It's a fine way of gaining balance after a hectic day. This recipe makes plenty of soup so that you will have leftovers for the next day.

1 cup long-grain rice
2 cups diced (1 inch), boned chicken meat
4 cloves garlic, crushed
1 yellow onion, cut into quarters
1 tablespoon sliced fresh ginger
1 teaspoon ground black pepper
1 tablespoon salt, or to taste
1 2/3 cups clear chicken stock
3 quarts water
1 cup thinly sliced green onion

Combine all the ingredients except the green onion in a large kettle and bring to a boil. Lower the heat to medium-low, cover, and simmer for 1 1/2 hours, stirring now and then.

Serve garnished with green onion.

Serves 6.

This is the hit soup that never misses its target. In Burma's major cities, shops selling this soup are as abundant as cafes are in France. Be sure to use canned coconut milk from Thailand or the Philippines. It would be a disaster to use sweet, coconut milk–based piña colada mix, which an American friend of mine once did.

It is hard work making this soup, so it is best to make a large amount when you do. This recipe assures everyone a second helping and leftovers, too.

One 3- to 4-pound chicken
1 teaspoon salt
1 tablespoon ground turmeric
1 cup plus 1 tablespoon vegetable oil
2 large yellow onions, finely chopped
8 cloves garlic, pounded in a mortar
1 tablespoon finely chopped fresh ginger
1 teaspoon paprika
1/2 teaspoon ground black pepper
6 tablespoons fish sauce, or to taste
4 quarts plus 3 cups water
1/2 cup roasted and skinned peanuts,
    finely ground in a blender or nut grinder
1 cup chana dal powder
4 cups canned coconut milk
24 shallots
2 pounds fresh or dried Chinese chow mein noodles
    (1/8 inch thick)

G A R N I S H E S
6 eggs, hard cooked, shelled,, and cut into
    1/4-inch-thick slices
1 cup chopped fresh cilantro
1 cup chopped green onion
6 limes, quartered
1/2 cup fish sauce
1/2 cup crushed dried red chile pepper

Bone and skin the chicken and remove any visible fat. Cut the meat into 1/2-inch cubes and place in a bowl. Add 1/2 teaspoon of the salt and 1 1/2 teaspoons of the turmeric. With your hands, mix the ingredients together thoroughly. Let stand for 15 minutes.

Heat the 1 cup oil in a large kettle over medium heat. Add the onions and the remaining 1 1/2 teaspoons turmeric and sauté until onions are translucent, about 5 minutes. Add the chicken, garlic, ginger, paprika, black pepper, and the remaining 1/2 teaspoon salt. Stir well and cook for 5 minutes. Add the fish sauce and cook, stirring, for 1 minute. Add the 4 quarts water and bring to a boil. Lower the heat, cover, and simmer gently for 30 minutes.

Place the ground peanuts in a bowl, add 1 cup of the remaining water, and mix well. Place the chana dal powder in a bowl, add the remaining 2 cups water, and mix well. Add the peanut and chana dal powder mixes to the kettle. Stir gently to mix with the other ingredients. Cover and simmer for 30 minutes. Add the coconut milk and simmer, covered, for 30 minutes, stirring frequently. Mix in the shallots.

Twenty minutes before the soup is ready, bring a large saucepan filled with water to a boil. Add the 1 tablespoon oil and the noodles and cook until just tender, 3 to 4 minutes for fresh noodles and about 10 minutes for dried. Drain well and set aside.

To serve the soup, put all the garnishes in separate bowls and place them in the middle of the table. Put approximately 1 1/2 cups of noodles in each large individual soup bowl. Ladle in enough soup to cover the noodles. Be sure to be generous with the chicken pieces. Let your guests garnish their own servings. I suggest about 1 tablespoon egg slices, a generous pinch of cilantro and green onion and a good squeeze of lime juice. Chile pepper and fish sauce can be added to taste. Provide forks and large spoons for eating this dish.

Serves 8.

Kyarzan Chet

*Bean Thread Noodle Soup with Chicken, Bean Curd,
Dried Lilies, Black Mushrooms, and Black Fungus*

This soup is often served on ceremonial occasions. A Burmese will take great pride in searching out the best version he can find to dazzle his guests and outdo his rivals. Although kyarzan chet *can be found in many Burmese soup stalls, the commercial soups cannot compare to their homemade cousins. Here is a classic. Remember that it is not the formula but rather the touch that is all important.*

5 ounces bean thread noodles, soaked in cold water to cover
  for 1 hour, drained, and snipped into 3-inch lengths
3 1/2 ounces dried bean curd sheets, soaked in warm water
  to cover for 1 hour, drained, and torn into
  1-inch by 2-inch pieces
4 ounces dried lily flowers soaked in warm water to cover
  for 30 minutes, drained, and each thread tied into a knot
4 ounces dried black fungus soaked in warm water to cover
  for 30 minutes, and drained
5 ounces dried black mushrooms, soaked in warm water to
  cover for 1 hour, drained, and cut in half
3 stalks lemongrass
1/2 cup vegetable oil
1 1/2 pounds boned chicken meat (preferably leg and thigh
  meat), cut into 1/2-inch cubes
1 yellow onion, finely chopped
6 cloves garlic, finely chopped
1 tablespoon finely minced fresh ginger
1/4 teaspoon ground turmeric
1 tablespoon paprika
1/2 teaspoon ground black pepper
1/2 cup fish sauce
4 cups clear chicken stock
4 quarts plus 2 cups water

GARNISHES
1 cup chopped green onion
1/2 cup finely chopped fresh cilantro
1/2 cup crushed dried red chile pepper
5 limes, cut into quarters

Soak and cut all the dried ingredients as directed; set aside.

Pound the heads of the lemongrass stalks lightly with a kitchen mallet or hammer. Fold each stalk into a 3-inch-long loop and tie it with kitchen string; set aside.

Heat the oil in a large pot over medium heat. Add the chicken, onion, garlic, ginger, turmeric, paprika, and black pepper. Sauté until the chicken and onion are light brown. Add the tied lemongrass, fish sauce, chicken stock, and water. Bring to a boil, cover, and simmer for 10 minutes.

Add the reserved noodles, bean curd, lily flowers, black fungus, and mushrooms. Simmer, covered, for 15 minutes.

Ladle the soup into individual serving bowls. Sprinkle each serving with a generous pinch of green onions and cilantro. Pass the peppers and lime quarters for diners to add to taste. Serve the soup very hot.

Serves 10.

Mohingar
Fish Soup with Noodles

Mohingar *is a passion of the Burmese people. Almost every morning, the urge to have this soup seems to grip every Burmese. But they will also eat it any time of the day, anywhere—in their homes, at a food stall, purchased from itinerant vendors. The latter are mobile cooks who make their rounds of the neighborhoods on foot, carrying a pole on their shoulders. On one end there is a big pot full of soup with a small charcoal burner beneath; at the other end hang the cooked noodles, bowls, and other accessories. A favorite pastime of neighbors is sitting around the vendor and trading gossip and small talk while eating the soup.*

Although whole, fresh catfish is the fish to use when making this soup, they are difficult to handle because they are slimy and the sharp fins can nick you quite easily. I prefer to use catfish fillets if I am lucky enough to find them at the market. Or I substitute other filleted fish such as snapper, cod, haddock, halibut, or grouper. Some days, if I don't feel like fussing with a trip to the Chinatown fish markets, I walk to the corner store and buy canned light tuna chunks.

In Burma the essential ingredient for mohingar *is the inner soft stem of the banana tree trunk, which is called* ngapyawoo. *The trunk is made up of many fibrous layers formed in continuous concentric circles. The outer skin is woody, but if you peel the layers off until you reach the soft inner substance, which is perhaps three inches in diameter, the tree reveals its secret heart. It is cut into half-inch-thick slices and added to the soup.*

The Los Angeles area is the only place I know of in the United States where banana trees grow in abundance. When I was living there, my friend and I would drive around secluded areas in his pickup in search of them. As soon as we found one, he would jump out, hastily cut it with his axe, and haul it back to the truck, and we would speed off like commandoes on a dangerous mission. Truthfully though, the soup is still wonderful without it.

I have used Japanese somen *noodles for this recipe because they look and taste very similar to the traditional Burmese noodles used in* mohingar, *which, to my knowledge, are unavailable in the West.*

4 pounds catfish, red snapper, halibut, cod,
   haddock, or grouper fillet
1 tablespoon salt
1 tablespoon ground turmeric
3 stalks fresh lemongrass
1/2 cup roasted and skinned peanuts
1/2 cup long-grain white rice
1 cup plus 1 tablespoon vegetable oil
4 yellow onions, finely chopped
8 garlic cloves, pounded in a mortar
1 tablespoon finely chopped fresh ginger
1 tablespoon paprika
1 teaspoon ground black pepper
1/2 cup fish sauce, or to taste
4 quarts plus 2 cups water
1 cup mung beans, boiled in water to cover
   until tender, drained, and mashed
12 shallots
1 package (14 ounces) Japanese *somen* noodles

GARNISHES
6 eggs, hard cooked, shelled, and cut into
   1/4-inch-thick slices
1 cup chopped fresh cilantro
1 cup chopped green onion
6 limes, quartered
1/2 cup fish sauce
1/2 cup crushed dried red chile pepper

Remove any bones that may remain in the fillets. Cut the fillets into 1-inch cubes. Place in a bowl and add 1 1/2 teaspoons each of the salt and turmeric. With your hands, mix well and let stand for 15 minutes.

Pound the heads of the lemongrass stalks lightly with a kitchen mallet or hammer. Fold each stalk into a 3-inch-long loop and tie it with kitchen string. This step makes the aroma come out nicely. Set the lemongrass aside.

Place the peanuts in a blender and pulverize until finely ground; do not allow a paste to form. Set aside. Heat a small, dry skillet over medium-high heat. Add the rice and stir until browned but not scorched, about 5 minutes. Transfer the rice to a blender and pulverize it until it is the consistency of fine sand. Set aside.

Heat the 1 cup oil in a large kettle over medium heat. Add the onions and the remaining 1 1/2 teaspoons turmeric and sauté until the onions are translucent, about 5 minutes. Add the fish, garlic, ginger, lemongrass, paprika, black pepper, fish sauce, and the remaining 1 1/2 teaspoons salt. Stir well and cook for 5 minutes.

Add the 4 quarts water, raise the heat and bring to a boil. Lower the heat to a simmer. Mix the reserved ground nuts with 1 cup of the remaining water. Mix the ground rice with the remaining 1 cup water. Add mung bean paste and peanut and rice powder mixtures to the kettle. Stir gently to mix with the other ingredients. Cover and simmer gently for 30 minutes, stirring frequently. Mix in the shallots.

Meanwhile, bring a large pot of water to a boil. Add the noodles and the 1 tablespoon oil and boil until the noodles are tender, about 5 minutes. Drain and set aside.

To serve, put all the garnishes in separate bowls and place them in the middle of the table. Put a good-sized mound of noodles in each large individual soup bowl. Ladle in enough soup to cover the noodles. Be sure to include some fish pieces. Let your guests garnish their own servings. I suggest about 1 tablespoon egg slices, a generous pinch of cilantro and green onion, and a good squeeze of lime juice. Chile pepper and fish sauce can be added to taste. Provide forks and large spoons for eating this dish.

Serves 6 to 8.

C hicken used to cause conflict within me. I loved watching the birds roaming freely in our backyard in Rangoon, yet their meat was my favorite. Now that I have lived in America for quite a few years, I am more at ease with that earlier sentiment. When I buy a chicken here, it has no life with which I am familiar. It is just another "faceless" food among many thousands sold daily.

Back home I would have to point out a live chicken to let the seller know which one I wanted. In Burma's markets, chickens are sold live and then slaughtered and cleaned on the spot. The hardest part is the choosing. The chickens are kept in bamboo cages and the buyer must pick a healthy one that is often also the most beautiful. Thus, the chosen chicken's personality remains in your mind.

The free-range chickens we pay so dearly for here in America are probably closest in flavor to Burmese chicken.

The train from Rangoon to Mandalay makes some sixty stops during the journey. At the stations one can get any kind of food under the sun, from sparrows to fireflies. But out of the enormous selection, the very first thing I always used to pick to oblige my rumbling stomach was this fried chicken. It's so "finger lickin' good" that my southern friends call me Colonel Taik.

The manner in which the chicken is cut up for this recipe is how the Burmese most often cut chicken for cooking.

> One 3- to 4-pound chicken
> 1 tablespoon salt
> 1/2 teaspoon ground turmeric
> 4 cups vegetable oil

Skin the whole chicken. Cut the wings from the body. Clip off the wing tips and cut the wings in half at the joint. Remove the legs and cut each leg crosswise into 4 pieces. Separate the breast from the back; cut the breast and the rack in half lengthwise, then cut each half crosswise into 4 pieces. Place the chicken pieces in a bowl and sprinkle with the salt and turmeric. With your hands, mix the ingredients thoroughly and let stand for 30 minutes.

Heat the oil in a large frying pan over high heat. Add the chicken pieces and fry, turning once, until golden brown on both sides, about 10 minutes per side. Remove with a slotted utensil to paper towels to drain.

Serve hot or at room temperature.

Serves 4.

Kyethar Ahcho Kyaw
Caramelized Chicken with Cilantro

Here is one of my mother's gems. The way the caramelized sugar blends with the garlic and cilantro is truly exceptional.

One 3- to 4-pound chicken
1/2 teaspoon ground turmeric
1 teaspoon salt
2 tablespoons finely minced garlic
1 teaspoon finely chopped fresh ginger
2 tablespoons light soy sauce
2 egg yolks
1 cup all-purpose flour
1 1/2 cups vegetable oil
2 tablespoons granulated sugar
1 tablespoon finely chopped fresh cilantro
1 tablespoon distilled white vinegar
1 teaspoon crushed dried red chile pepper

Cut the chicken into pieces as described for Fried Chicken on page 62. In a large bowl, place the chicken, turmeric, salt, 1 tablespoon of the garlic, ginger, soy sauce, and egg yolks. With your hands, mix the ingredients thoroughly. Cover and refrigerate for 1 hour.

Add the flour to the chicken mixture and mix it in thoroughly with your hands. Cover and return the chicken to the refrigerator for 3 hours.

Heat the oil in a large frying pan over medium-high heat. Add the chicken and fry, turning once, until golden brown on both sides, about 10 minutes per side. Remove the chicken with a slotted utensil to paper towels to drain.

Remove all but 2 tablespoons of the oil from the pan. Reheat the oil in the pan over medium-low heat. Sprinkle the sugar and the remaining 1 tablespoon garlic over the oil. Heat, stirring often, until the sugar liquifies, thickens, and then darkens. Add the chicken, cilantro, vinegar, and chile pepper. Stir gently to coat the chicken pieces on all sides. Serve at once.

Serves 4.

During my boarding school days, my mother kept me well supplied with this dish as a tasty contrast to the school's cuisine. Eating it with steamed rice gives you full satisfaction. Or you can sprinkle it generously on toast. It's unbelievably good.

You can also make this dish using leftover cooked turkey. You will need about 3 cups shredded meat. Both versions will keep in an airtight jar in the refrigerator for several weeks.

One 4-pound chicken
2 large yellow onions
1 cup vegetable oil
1/2 teaspoon ground turmeric
8 cloves garlic, thinly sliced
2 teaspoons salt
3 tablespoons crushed dried red chile pepper

Place the chicken in a large saucepan with water to cover. Bring to a boil, lower the heat, cover with lid slightly ajar, and cook until the chicken is tender, about 30 minutes. Remove the chicken from the pan. When it is cool enough to handle, skin and bone the chicken and shred the meat into stringlike pieces.

While the chicken is cooking, cut the onions in half vertically and then slice the halves thinly to form crescent-shaped fans. Heat the oil in a frying pan over medium heat. Add the onions and turmeric and cook until the onions begin to color. Add the garlic and continue to cook until the onions and garlic are golden brown, about 6 minutes. Remove the onions and garlic with a slotted spoon and set aside. Reserve the oil in the pan.

Add the chicken shreds to the reserved oil and cook over medium heat, stirring frequently, until they begin to brown, about 10 minutes. Drain off the oil from the pan. Add the reserved onions and garlic, salt, and chile pepper to the chicken and stir well. Cook over medium-low heat, stirring, for 10 minutes.

Serves 4.

Kyethar Susie Kyaw
Diced Chicken with Crushed Chilies

One of the rare Burmese dishes that is prepared in the stir-fry style of Chinese cooks.

2 cups diced (1 inch), boned chicken meat
1 1/2 tablespoons fish sauce
3/4 teaspoon ground turmeric
1 large yellow onion
1 cup plus 3 tablespoons vegetable oil
3 cloves garlic, diced
1 tablespoon crushed dried red chile pepper
2 green onions, julienned

In a bowl, place the chicken, fish sauce, and 1/4 teaspoon of the turmeric. With your hands, mix the ingredients thoroughly and let stand for about 20 minutes.

Cut the onion in half vertically and then slice the halves thinly to form crescent-shaped fans. Heat 1 cup oil in a frying pan over medium heat. Add the onion and 1/4 teaspoon of the turmeric and fry until golden brown, about 6 minutes. Remove the onion with a slotted spoon and set aside to use as a garnish.

Heat 3 tablespoons oil in a large skillet over medium heat. Add the garlic, chile, and the remaining 1/4 teaspoon of turmeric and sauté until the garlic is light brown, 2 to 3 minutes. Add the chicken and green onions and stir-fry until the chicken is tender, about 5 minutes.

Remove the chicken to a serving dish and sprinkle with the reserved onions. Serve immediately.

Serves 4.

Kyethar Kabut Kyaw
Sautéed Curried Chicken with Bell Peppers

After my introduction to Mexican food in San Francisco, I found that serving this dish with tortillas was a splendid idea. Un burrito hecho en Burmania.

2 cups diced (1 inch), boned chicken meat
1 1/2 teaspoons salt
1/4 teaspoon ground turmeric
1 tablespoon ground cumin
1/4 teaspoon ground black pepper
1 cup sour cream
1/4 cup vegetable oil
1 tomato, thinly sliced
2 small yellow onions, cut into thin rings
1 tablespoon distilled white vinegar
1 large bell pepper, seeded, deveined, and
   cut into 1-inch squares

In a bowl, place the chicken, salt, turmeric, cumin, black pepper, and sour cream. With your hands, mix the ingredients thoroughly and let stand for 1 hour.

Heat the oil in a large frying pan over medium-high heat. Add the chicken and sauté until almost tender, about 4 minutes. Add the tomato, onion, vinegar, and bell pepper. Sauté, mixing well, until the chicken is cooked through, 3 to 4 minutes.

Serves 4.

A popular recipe in Burmese households when time is short and people are hungry. Only the method is simple, not the taste.

> One 3- to 4-pound chicken
> 1 teaspoon salt
> $1/2$ teaspoon ground turmeric
> $1/4$ cup vegetable oil
> 1 yellow onion, finely chopped
> 1 teaspoon paprika
> 2 tablespoons fish sauce
> 2 cups water

Cut the chicken into pieces as described for Fried Chicken on page 62. In a large bowl, place the chicken, salt, and turmeric. With your hands, mix the ingredients thoroughly and let stand for 10 minutes.

Heat the oil in a medium-sized saucepan over medium-high heat. Add the chicken, onion, paprika, and fish sauce and sauté for 5 minutes. Add the water, raise the heat, and bring to a boil. Lower the heat and simmer uncovered, stirring frequently, until the liquid is reduced by two thirds and a film of oil appears on the surface. (The world *sepyan* means "the return of oil.")

Serves 4.

Masala Kyethar Ghin
Baked Chicken with Sour Cream or Yogurt

Marinating chicken meat in sour cream or yogurt before cooking makes the meat extremely tender and moist. The Burmese learned this method from the Indians many generations ago.

2 whole chicken breasts, halved lengthwise or
   4 leg-and-thigh pieces
$1/2$ cup sour cream or plain yogurt
1 $1/2$ teaspoons salt
$1/2$ teaspoon ground turmeric
2 tablespoons ground cumin
1 teaspoon paprika
1 teaspoon ground cardamom
$1/4$ vegetable oil
1 lime

Remove the skin from the chicken pieces. With a sharp knife, make 3 slashes 1 $1/2$ inches apart and $1/8$ inch deep on each breast piece or on both sides of each leg-and-thigh piece.

Put the chicken pieces in a shallow bowl. Add all the remaining ingredients except the lime. With your hands, mix well to coat the chicken evenly. Cover and refrigerate at least 10 hours or as long as overnight.

Preheat the oven to 350° F. Arrange the chicken pieces on a baking sheet and bake for 30 minutes.

Remove the chicken from the oven and squeeze the lime over the top just before serving.

Serves 4.

Kalapei Kyetharhin

Chicken Curry with Yellow Split Peas

Two cooking techniques—for preparing curry and for preparing soup—are used for making this dish. They result in a hearty gravy to liven up steamed rice.

1 1/2 cups yellow split peas
5 cups water
One 3- to 4-pound chicken
1 tablespoon salt
1 teaspoon ground turmeric
1/4 cup vegetable oil
1 yellow onion, finely chopped
2 bay leaves
1 tablespoon ground cumin
1/8 teaspoon ground cloves
1/8 teaspoon ground nutmeg
1 teaspoon paprika

Rinse the split peas in cold water; drain. In a saucepan, combine 4 cups of the water and the peas. Bring to a boil and boil gently until the peas are half-cooked and still hold their shape. Pour off all of the water except for 1 cup. Set the split peas aside.

Meanwhile, cut the chicken into pieces as described for Fried Chicken on page 62. In a large bowl, place the chicken, salt, and turmeric. With your hands, mix the ingredients together thoroughly and let stand for about 10 minutes.

Heat the oil in a medium-sized saucepan over medium heat. Add the onion and bay leaves and sauté until the onion begins to soften, 3 minutes. Add the chicken, cumin, cloves, nutmeg, and paprika. Cook, stirring, 5 minutes.

Add the remaining 1 cup water, cover, and simmer for 20 minutes. Add the reserved split peas, cover, and simmer for 15 minutes.

Serves 4.

Kyethar Ohno Hin

Coconut Chicken Curry

Although somewhat similar to Coconut Chicken Soup (page 50), this dish is meant to be served with rice as a main course.

One 3- to 4-pound chicken
2 teaspoons salt
1 teaspoon ground turmeric
1/4 cup vegetable oil
2 yellow onions, finely chopped
3 garlic cloves, finely minced
1 teaspoon paprika
1/4 teaspoon ground red chile pepper
1 cup water
2 cups canned coconut milk

Cut the chicken into pieces as described for Fried Chicken on page 62. In a large bowl, place the chicken, salt, and turmeric. With your hands, mix the ingredients together thoroughly and let stand for 10 minutes.

Heat the oil in a 2-quart saucepan over medium heat. Add the onions and garlic and sauté until translucent, about 5 minutes. Add the chicken, paprika, and chile. Cook, stirring, for 5 minutes. Add the water and coconut milk, cover with the lid slightly ajar, and simmer for 30 minutes.

Serves 4.

People who know very little about Burmese cuisine often ask me whether we use a lot of lemongrass in our cooking as the Thai do. In general we don't, but one does find lemongrass used more often in the southeast districts of Burma, which border Thailand. My aunt from Moulmein, a large city in that area, was particularly fond of cooking this aromatic dish.

One 3- to 4-pound chicken
1 1/2 teaspoons salt
1/2 teaspoon ground turmeric
2 stalks fresh lemongrass
1/4 cup vegetable oil
2 yellow onions, chopped
2 cloves garlic, minced
1 teaspoon paprika
1 cup water

Cut the chicken into pieces as described for Fried Chicken on page 62. In a large bowl, place the chicken, salt, and turmeric. With your hands, mix the ingredients together thoroughly and let stand for 15 minutes.

Pound the heads of the lemongrass stalks lightly with a kitchen mallet or hammer. Fold each stalk into a 3-inch-long loop and tie it with kitchen string; set aside.

Heat the oil in a large 2-inch-deep frying pan over medium heat. Add the onions, garlic, and paprika and sauté until the onions are translucent, about 5 minutes. Add the chicken and lemongrass. Cook, stirring, for 5 minutes. Add the water, cover, and simmer for 30 minutes.

Serves 4.

Kyethar Peinathar Hin
Chicken Curry with Fenugreek

Even though there are other spices in this dish, the inclusion of a small amount of fenugreek dominates the curry's flavor and aroma. It contributes a lemony accent without being sour. During my early days in America, my mother and I thought fenugreek was as rare as moon dust. We had small packages of it sent from Burma, and we never knew what is was called in English. One day we took a sample of it to an Indian merchant. The man took one sniff and pointed toward an enormous barrel labeled methi. *Indeed, America has everything!*

One 3- to 4-pound chicken
2 yellow onions, chopped
1 tablespoon ground fenugreek
2 tablespoons ground cumin
1 tablespoon ground coriander
$1/2$ teaspoon ground cardamom
$1/2$ teaspoon ground turmeric
2 bay leaves
2 teaspoons salt
1 tablespoon distilled white vinegar
$1/4$ cup vegetable oil
1 cup water

Cut the chicken in pieces as described for Fried Chicken on page 62. In a large bowl, place the chicken with all the remaining ingredients except the oil and water. With your hands, mix the ingredients together thoroughly and let stand for 1 hour.

Heat the oil in a medium-sized saucepan over medium heat. Add the chicken and sauté for 5 minutes. Add the water and raise the heat to high. Bring to a boil, lower the heat, cover, and simmer until the liquid is reduced to $1/4$ cup, about 30 minutes.

Serves 4.

Kyethar Katalet
Chicken Cutlet

Most Burmese doctors who were my father's contemporaries did their postgraduate studies in England. As a young man I heard stories about how tiresome it was for them to eat English-style meals day in and day out. One might think that they'd had enough of that fare, but strangely, when they came back to Burma, they often treated themselves to English dinners adapted to suit Burmese taste. We call this type of cooking "made in Burma English food," and many English friends have found it interesting and different. This recipe, created by my mother, has been in our family ever since my father returned from his first trip to England.

4 cups ground chicken meat
1 green onion, thinly sliced
1 yellow onion, finely chopped
1 teaspoon minced garlic
1 teaspoon chopped fresh cilantro
1 teaspoon salt
1/2 teaspoon ground black pepper
2 egg yolks
3 tablespoons plus about 2 cups all-purpose flour
1/2 cup vegetable oil

In a large bowl, place the chicken, green and yellow onions, garlic, cilantro, salt, pepper, egg yolks, and the 3 tablespoons flour. With your hands, mix the ingredients together thoroughly and let stand for 1 hour.

Form the chicken mixture into round patties about the size of a hamburger. Dust the patties generously with the 2 cups flour. Heat the oil in a large frying pan over medium-low heat. Add the chicken patties and cook, turning once, until nicely browned and cooked through, about 3 minutes per side. Alternatively, omit the flour for dusting and the oil and cook the patties on a grill rack over a charcoal fire.

Serves 4.

Kyethar Pyokekyaw
Chicken Stew

To eat this stew is to eat Burmese history whole. Imagine a dish created by a Burmese cook to impress an Englishman and his Chinese wife. During British colonial rule in Burma, many cooks were trained to prepare food in the European manner by their British employers. I remember that my mother employed a man whose father had cooked for British officials. Although he could barely read English, he did have some verbal grasp of the language. One day my mother asked him if he needed anything for the kitchen. He grabbed an empty bottle of Worcestershire sauce, turned the bottle upside down, and said, "Shake bottle is out, madame."

One 3- to 4-pound chicken
3 tablespoons Worcestershire sauce
3 tablespoons light soy sauce
$1/4$ teaspoon ground black pepper
2 tablespoons vegetable oil
1 cup water
2 tablespoons butter

Cut the chicken in pieces as described for Fried Chicken on page 62. In a large bowl, place the chicken, Worcestershire sauce, soy sauce, and black pepper. With your hands, mix the ingredients together thoroughly and let stand for 30 minutes.

Heat the oil in a 2-quart saucepan over medium heat. Add the chicken and sauté for 5 minutes. Add the water and butter, cover, and cook until the chicken is tender, about 30 minutes.

Serves 4.

Bairthar Sepyan
Duck Curry

Duck prepared in a curry sauce is fantastic. Come to think of it, one hardly finds duck curry dishes in any restaurants, including Burmese ones, of which there are very few in America.

> One 3- to 4-pound Long Island duck
> 2 yellow onions, diced
> 4 cloves garlic, finely chopped
> 1 teaspoon finely minced fresh ginger
> 1 teaspoon paprika
> 1 1/2 teaspoons salt
> 1 teaspoon distilled white vinegar
> 1/2 teaspoon ground cayenne pepper
> 1 tablespoon fish sauce
> 1/2 cup minced tomato
> 1/4 cup vegetable oil
> 1 3/4 cups water
> 2 tablespoons ground cumin

Skin the duck and remove all visible fat. Cut the duck in pieces in the same manner the chicken is cut for Fried Chicken on page 62. In a large bowl, place the duck, onions, garlic, ginger, paprika, salt, vinegar, cayenne, fish sauce, tomato, and oil. With your hands, mix the ingredients together thoroughly and let stand for 30 minutes.

In a medium-sized saucepan over medium heat, cook the duck and 1/4 cup of water until the water evaporates, about 5 minutes. Add the remaining 1 1/2 cups water and bring to a boil. Lower the heat, cover, and simmer, stirring frequently, until the liquid is reduced by three quarters and a film of oil appears on the surface, about 40 minutes.

Add the cumin, stir well, and simmer for 5 minutes.

Serves 4.

Bairthar Ghin
Roast Duck

When I tell my guests that I am serving roast duck for dinner, they are always exulted by the announcement. But I have rarely eaten duck at the homes of my American friends. I think most people equate duck with fat. I can't argue with that, but there are two good ways to rid the fowl of fat—by removing the skin and any visible fat or by steaming. To experience this delightful meat, one must be able to sink the idea of calories well below the level of consciousness. Enjoy.

> One 3- to 4-pound Long Island duck
> 2 tablespoons Worcestershire sauce
> 2 tablespoons light soy sauce
> 1 teaspoon granulated sugar
> 1 tablespoon cornstarch, dissolved in 2 tablespoons water

In a large bowl, combine the duck, Worcestershire sauce, soy sauce, and sugar. Turn the duck to coat well and let stand for 2 hours.

Remove the duck from the marinade, reserving the marinade. Fill a steamer pan with water to a depth of 1 1/2 inches. Place the duck, breast side up, on a steamer rack above the water. Cover, bring the water to a gentle boil, and steam the duck for 30 minutes. Skim off and discard the fat from the steaming juices; reserve the juices.

Preheat the oven to 400° F. Transfer the duck to a 1-inch-deep baking pan and brush the duck well with the reserved marinade. Roast uncovered for 15 minutes; lower the heat to 350° F and roast until the meat is tender when pierced with a thin metal skewer or until a leg moves freely when shaken, about 40 minutes.

Remove the duck to a cutting board. Skim off and discard any fat from the cooking juices in the pan. Transfer the cooking juices to a small saucepan, along with the reserved steaming juices. Bring to a simmer over medium heat, add the cornstarch mixture, and cook, stirring, until slightly thickened, 2 to 3 minutes. Keep warm.

Cut the wings off the duck. Cut the leg-and-thigh sections off the duck and divide each section at the joint. Cut the breast away from the back. Cut the breast in half lengthwise and then cut each half crosswise into 2 pieces. Cut the back in half lengthwise. Arrange the duck pieces on a serving platter and top with the warm gravy.

Serves 4.

This Rangoon dish is usually cooked during the winter season, which runs from November to February. Winter in Burma is like a cool summer day in most of the United States.

Steamed rice and vegetables will complement the pleasure of this homey, succulent dish.

One 3- to 4-pound Long Island duck
1 tablespoon minced garlic
3 tablespoons light soy sauce
1 tablespoon dark soy sauce
1 tablespoon Asian sesame oil
1/2 teaspoon salt
1/4 teaspoon ground black pepper
1/2 teaspoon granulated sugar
1/2 cup chopped celery
1 yellow onion, cut into quarters
1 tablespoon cornstarch, dissolved in 2 tablespoons water

Remove the loose fat from the cavity of the duck. In a small bowl, mix together the garlic, 1 tablespoon of the light soy sauce, dark soy sauce, sesame oil, salt, pepper, and sugar. Rub the duck inside and out with the mixture. Let the duck stand for 1 hour.

Fill a steamer pan with water to a depth of 1 1/2 inches. Stuff the cavity of the duck with the celery and onion. Place the duck, breast side up, in a 1-inch-deep flameproof dish or pan and place on the steamer rack above the water. Cover, bring the water to a gentle boil, and steam until the duck is tender when pierced with a thin metal skewer, about 1 hour.

Preheat the broiler. Remove the dish or pan from the steamer and brush the duck with the remaining 2 tablespoons light soy sauce. Broil the duck for 2 to 3 minutes, or until the skin is brown and crisp.

Remove the duck to a cutting board. Skim off and discard any fat from the cooking juices in the pan. Transfer the cooking juices to a small saucepan. Bring to a simmer over medium heat, add the cornstarch mixture, and cook, stirring, until slightly thickened, 2 to 3 minutes. Keep warm.

Cut the wings off the duck. Cut the leg-and-thigh section off the duck and divide each section at the joint. Cut the breast away from the back. Cut the breast in half lengthwise and then cut each half crosswise into 2 pieces. Cut the back in half lengthwise. Arrange all the duck pieces on a serving platter and top with the warm gravy.

Serves 4.

Americans often asked me, "Do people in Burma eat meat?" They know that Burma is a Buddhist country, so they assume that the people abstain from meat. Their confusion is understandable, since not killing animals is one of the five precepts laid down by Buddha. But Buddha never said a word about consuming animal flesh.

Doesn't the eating of meat rise from the killing of animals? Of course, but the thought behind that question is as fruitless as the thoughts of a drowning man who regrets that he didn't take swimming lessons. The Buddha himself ate meat; so do Buddhist monks and Burmese Buddhists. There are no rules governing it. But there are three choices that each person can make. He or she can eat *punthagu* meat, which is meat that comes from animals whose deaths were neither witnessed nor their suffering cries during slaughter heard. This is exactly the sort of meat one buys in the supermarket. If a person detests the killing part but still likes to eat meat, then he or she can choose to eat the meat of animals who died accidentally or from natural causes. And the third choice is to become a vegetarian.

The Burmese do not raise cattle for consumption. Most beef comes from retired working livestock, which makes the meat tough and the price high because of scarcity. There are also some grateful, prosperous farmers who don't need to sell their cows for meat but instead give them a sort of amnesty. They brand the cows with a mark stating that they are free to roam. But most cows are sold and end up on dinner plates.

Because our mixed population includes people of Chinese and Indian ethnicity, pork, goat meat, and mutton are more often consumed than beef. The spices we use are also a reflection of the various cultures living in the country. Long simmering is required for all types of meat, however, due to their general toughness.

The amount of meat the Burmese consume with their meal is inconsequential in comparison to the amounts of steak people consume in the West. A pound of meat, some vegetables, and rice is easily shared by a very large, even extended Burmese family.

Ahmai Naut
Beef Curry

It is most fitting to include this dish at a traditional, formal Burmese dinner. Coconut Rice (page 195) is generally served with this curry.

2 pounds boneless beef stew meat (about 2-inch pieces)
1 1/2 teaspoons salt
1/2 teaspoon ground turmeric
1 teaspoon paprika
2 cups chopped tomato
1 yellow onion, finely chopped
1 teaspoon finely minced fresh ginger
1 tablespoon finely minced fresh cilantro
1/2 teaspoon ground cayenne pepper
1/4 cup vegetable oil
6 cups water

In a bowl, combine all the ingredients except the water. With your hands, mix the ingredients together thoroughly and let stand for 30 minutes.

Transfer the beef mixture to a medium-sized saucepan and place over medium heat. Cook, stirring, until the beef is lightly browned, about 3 minutes. Add the water, cover, and simmer until the liquid is reduced to about 1/2 cup and the oil begins to appear on the surface, about 1 1/4 hours. If the meat needs to cook longer, add a little water and continue to simmer until tender.

Serves 4.

Ahmaithar Ahloo Kala Hin
Beef Curry with Potatoes and Spices

The Burmese eat meat for its flavor, while rice is consumed as filler. A quarter of a pound of beef with a tangy sauce is ample to complement a plateful of steamed rice. This dish is superb with Butter Rice with Raisins and Cashews (page 196).

2 pounds boneless beef stew meat (about 2-inch pieces)
3/4 teaspoon salt
1 teaspoon ground turmeric
1/2 cup vegetable oil
2 yellow onions, finely chopped
5 cloves garlic, minced
1 teaspoon finely minced fresh ginger
1/4 cup ground cumin
1 tablespoon ground coriander
1 tablespoon paprika
1 teaspoon ground cayenne pepper
1 teaspoon ground cardamom
1 tablespoon finely chopped fresh cilantro
4 medium-sized red potatoes, peeled and cut into quarters
5 cups water

In a bowl, place the beef, salt, and turmeric. With your hands, mix the ingredients together thoroughly. Heat the oil in a medium-sized pot over medium heat. Add the onions, garlic, and ginger and sauté until the onions begin to soften, 3 minutes. Add all the remaining ingredients except the potatoes and water, and sauté until the beef is lightly browned, about 5 minutes.

Add the water, cover, and simmer until the liquid is reduced by about three quarters. Add the potatoes and simmer until the potatoes are tender, about 20 minutes.

Serves 4.

Ahmaipauk Ahloo Hin

Ground Beef and Potato Curry

This dish is ideal for a last-minute dinner with friends.

> 2 pounds ground sirloin
> 1 1/2 teaspoons salt, or to taste
> 1/2 teaspoon ground turmeric
> 1 tablespoon ground cumin
> 1/4 cup vegetable oil
> 2 yellow onions, chopped
> 2 bay leaves
> 4 medium-sized red potatoes, peeled and cut into eighths
> 2 cups water

In a bowl, place the sirloin, salt, turmeric, and cumin. With your hands, mix the ingredients together thoroughly and set aside.

Heat the oil in a 2-inch-deep frying pan over medium heat. Add the onions and bay leaves and sauté until the onions begin to soften, 3 minutes. Add the potatoes and cook, stirring, for 3 minutes.

Add the water, cover, and simmer until the potatoes are almost cooked, 15 to 20 minutes.

Add the beef, stir well to mix in evenly, and cook, stirring, until the beef is cooked, about 5 minutes.

Serves 4.

Ahmaithar Ohno Hin
Coconut Beef Curry

In my book Visions of Shwedagon, *I told the story of my friendship with a man who was having such a run of bad luck, he sold some sheets of the corrugated metal roof on his house in order to make me a dinner. In a small town like his, beef is a very rare commodity. Once in awhile, if someone's cow is struck by a truck or dies of old age, the entire village will be able to buy beef. Naturally, the meat has to be sold quickly, within the day, as there is no refrigeration. It was quite a coincidence that beef was available the day I arrived. My friend's wife cooked this dish for me at the cost of covering from the elements. It is a memory that will stay with me forever.*

2 pounds boneless beef stew meat (about 2-inch pieces)
1 teaspoon salt
$1/2$ teaspoon ground turmeric
$1/4$ cup vegetable oil
1 yellow onion, finely chopped
1 tablespoon paprika
6 cups water
2 cups canned coconut milk

In a bowl, place the beef, salt, and turmeric. With your hands, mix the ingredients together thoroughly.

Heat the oil in a medium-sized saucepan over medium heat. Add the onion and sauté until it begins to soften, 3 minutes.

Add the beef and paprika and sauté until the meat is lightly browned, about 5 minutes. Add the water, cover, and simmer until the water is *nearly* evaporated, about 1 $1/4$ hours. Add the coconut milk, cover, and simmer for 10 minutes.

Serves 4.

Ahmaithar Pyoke Kyaw
Beef Roast Stew

The Burmese thrive on curry. Hardly a day goes by when a curry is not eaten. But at times, to get away from the heavy spices, they turn to a light-tasting dish like this one. This recipe also brings out the flavor of beef more than a curry does.

2 pounds boneless beef stew meat (about 2-inch pieces)
1/4 teaspoon ground turmeric
2 teaspoons fish sauce
2 tablespoons light soy sauce
1/4 teaspoon ground black pepper
1/4 cup vegetable oil
6 cups water

In a bowl, combine all the ingredients except the water; with your hands, mix the ingredients together thoroughly and let stand for 30 minutes.

Transfer the beef mixture to a medium-sized saucepan and place over medium heat. Cook, stirring, until the beef is lightly browned, about 5 minutes. Add the water, cover, and simmer until the liquid is reduced to 1/2 cup and the oil begins to appear on the surface. If the meat needs to cook longer, add a little water and continue to simmer until tender.

Serves 4.

Ahmaithar Kebat Kyaw
Stir-Fried Beef Kabob

Muslim Indians in Rangoon prepare kabob quite differently from their Middle Eastern coreligionists. After barbecuing the spiced beef cubes, they slide the meat off the skewers and stir-fry it in a very hot pan with tomatoes, onions, and a little oil, cooking the mixture only until the onions just begin to soften. This recipe is a shortcut to that procedure, deleting the barbecuing step.

2 pounds flank steak
$1/2$ teaspoon ground turmeric
1 $1/2$ teaspoons salt, or to taste
3 tablespoon ground cumin
$1/4$ teaspoon ground black pepper
$1/4$ cup vegetable oil
2 medium-sized tomatoes, cut into eighths
2 medium-sized yellow onions, sliced into
  $1/2$-inch-thick rings

Cut the beef into strips 2 $1/2$ inches long, 1 inch wide, and $1/4$ inch thick. In a bowl, place the beef, turmeric, salt, cumin, and pepper. With your hands, mix the ingredients together thoroughly and let stand for 1 hour.

Heat the oil in a medium-sized frying pan over medium-high heat. Add the beef, tomatoes, and onions and stir-fry until the beef is tender, about 4 minutes.

Serves 4.

Ahmaithar Ghin
Spicy Barbecued Beef with Sour Cream

Due to the natural toughness of Burmese beef, we have to cook the meat in boiling water or marinate it in buttermilk, yogurt, or sour cream for many hours before barbecuing it. This recipe truly deserves to be tried with a choice cut such as London broil. I suggest serving it with Butter Rice with Raisins and Cashew Nuts (page 196), Cucumber-Onion Salad (page 146), and Yellow Split Pea Soup (page 42).

2 pounds London broil, cut into 2-inch cubes
1 teaspoon salt, or to taste
1 teaspoon ground turmeric
1 tablespoon paprika
1 tablespoon ground coriander
1 teaspoon ground cardamom
2 bay leaves
1 tablespoon paprika
5 tablespoons ground cumin
1/2 cup vegetable oil
1 1/2 cups sour cream
1 tablespoon fresh lemon juice

In a bowl, combine all the ingredients. With your hands, mix the ingredients together thoroughly. Cover and refrigerate overnight.

Prepare a fire in a charcoal grill. Thread the meat cubes onto metal skewers and arrange on the grill over medium coals. Grill until done to taste, 10 to 15 minutes on each side. Alternatively, arrange the skewers on a baking sheet and bake in a preheated 350° F oven for 30 minutes.

Serves 4.

Ahmaithar Kyaw
Fried Beef

This beef is unlike the soft, tender meat that results from cooking in the curry style. Instead it is a little on the chewy side, imparting a strong sense of texture. The Burmese have a real penchant for eating foods—from betel nut to custard apple—that have different physical qualities. Texture is everything for us. This dish is usually eaten with Coconut Rice (page 196) and some kind of pickle. I suggest Cauliflower Pickle (page 186).

3 pounds boneless beef stew meat (about 2-inch pieces)
1 1/2 teaspoons salt
1 teaspoon ground turmeric
4 cups vegetable oil

In a bowl, place the beef, salt, and turmeric. With your hands, mix the ingredients together thoroughly and let stand for 15 minutes.

Heat the oil in a 2-inch-deep skillet over medium heat. Add the beef and fry, turning once, until golden brown on both sides, about 8 minutes per side.

Serves 4.

The flavor of zucchini makes ground beef taste cool and sweet. Back home we prepared this dish with a vegetable called kha wei thee *and usually served it for lunch. Angled luffa squash will also work, but it must be peeled before stuffing. A little steamed rice and a tomato salad is all you need to round out the meal.*

4 zucchini, each about 6 inches long and
   4 inches in diameter
1 pound ground sirloin
1 yellow onion, finely minced
1/2 teaspoon ground black pepper
1 1/2 teaspoons fish sauce
1 teaspoon salt
1 tablespoon paprika
1 tablespoon all-purpose flour
1/4 cup vegetable oil
1/2 cup water

Cut the zucchini crosswise into 2-inch-long pieces. Carefully remove the pulp from center of each zucchini piece, leaving walls about 1/4 inch thick. Set the zucchini tubes aside.

In a bowl, place the sirloin, onion, pepper, fish sauce, salt, paprika, and flour. With your hands, mix the ingredients together thoroughly. Stuff the beef mixture into the zucchini tubes.

Heat the oil and water in a frying pan over medium heat. Add the stuffed zucchini and simmer gently, turning frequently, until the water evaporates and the oil appears on the surface, about 10 minutes. Reduce the heat to medium-low. Fry, stirring gently, for 5 minutes.

Serves 4.

Ahmaiou Hin
Tripe Curry

Like the French, the Burmese consider tripe a delicacy. When I was in Paris, I was thrilled to go to the open-air markets, which reminded me of the marketplaces in my homeland. There I fell in love with gras double, *a fully cooked tripe roll. In that city of gastronomical delights, I felt proud that my tripe curry cooked with their* gras double *was a hit with my Parisian friends.*

1 1/2 pounds honeycomb tripe, cut into
    pieces 2 inches long and 3/4 inch wide
3 tablespoons vegetable oil
1 yellow onion, finely chopped
4 cloves garlic, finely minced
1/4 teaspoon ground turmeric
1 teaspoon paprika
1 teaspoon salt
4 cups water

Fill a large saucepan with water and add the tripe. Bring to a boil and boil for 15 minutes. Drain and set aside.

Heat the oil in a medium-sized saucepan over medium heat. Add the onion, garlic, turmeric, and paprika and sauté until the onion begins to soften, 3 minutes. Add the salt and reserved tripe and cook, stirring, for 3 minutes. Add the water, cover, and simmer until the water is reduced to 1/2 cup and the tripe is tender, about 1 1/4 hours.

Serves 4.

Most Burmese pork curries are cooked in this provincial style. It is a simple cooking technique with a free spirit to it, much like that of a Matisse drawing. Now and then some distant relatives from a faraway district would turn up at our door. During their stay they would offer their services. And without hesitation we would always lead them to the kitchen where they would prepare savory country dishes. Our house cook always prayed for their return.

> 2 pounds boneless lean pork, cut into
>   pieces 2 inches long and 1 inch wide
> 1 yellow onion, finely chopped
> 1/2 teaspoon salt
> 1/2 teaspoon ground turmeric
> 1 1/2 teaspoons fish sauce
> 1 teaspoon finely minced fresh ginger
> 1 tablespoon paprika
> 3 tablespoons vegetable oil
> 6 cups water

In a bowl, place all the ingredients except the water. With your hands, mix the ingredients together thoroughly and let stand for 30 minutes.

Heat a medium-sized saucepan over medium-low heat. Add the pork and sprinkle with 2 tablespoons of the water. Cook, stirring often, until the meat is well browned, about 7 minutes. Add the water, cover, and simmer until the liquid is reduced to 1 cup and the oil begins to appear on the surface, 1 1/4 to 1 1/2 hours.

Serves 4.

Whetthar Buthee Hin
Pork Curry with Bottleneck Gourd

Combining pork with gourd in a curry is another country-style favorite. Families who live outside the city grow gourd plants on pergolas attached to their dwellings. This practice creates cool, shady areas that are pleasant places for families to escape to from the heat of the day. Burmese are fortunate that they have a fertile land and plenty of rain. There is no good reason for anyone to go hungry.

2 pounds boneless lean pork, cut into
   pieces 2 inches long and 1 inch wide
1 teaspoon salt
$1/2$ teaspoon ground turmeric
$1/4$ cup vegetable oil
1 yellow onion, finely chopped
4 cloves garlic, finely minced
1 tablespoon paprika
6 cups water
1 pound bottleneck gourds

In a bowl, place the pork, salt, and turmeric. With your hands, mix the ingredients together thoroughly and let stand for 10 minutes.

Heat the oil in a medium-sized saucepan over medium-low heat. Add the onion, garlic, and paprika and sauté until the onion begins to soften, 3 minutes. Add the pork and fry until the meat is nicely browned, about 5 minutes. Add the water, cover, and simmer until the liquid is reduced to about 1 cup, about 1 $1/4$ hours.

Meanwhile, peel the gourds. Cut in half lengthwise and scrape out and discard the seeds and pith. Cut the gourds into pieces 2 inches long and 1 inch thick. You should have about 4 cups. Add the gourd pieces to the saucepan, cover, and simmer until the gourd pieces are tender and translucent, about 8 minutes.

Serves 4.

Whetthar Myitchin Hin
Pork Curry with Bamboo Shoots

Bamboo, which grows abundantly all over Burma, is the country's most versatile plant. It is used in building homes, irrigating fields, making furniture and baskets, constructing scaffoldings, and so on, and the young shoots are eaten. Most Americans have been exposed only to canned bamboo shoots, which are rather mild in flavor and odorless. Fresh bamboo shoots, in contrast, have a pungent aroma and full flavor. They can be found already cleaned and ready for cooking in Asian markets, usually in buckets filled with water. They should be sought out for this dish to be authentic.

2 pounds lean pork, cut into
    pieces 2 inches long and 1 inch wide
1 teaspoon salt
1/2 teaspoon ground turmeric
1 tablespoon paprika
4 teaspoons vegetable oil
1 yellow onion, finely chopped
6 cups water
1 1/2 cups shredded fresh bamboo shoots, or 1 jar
    (13.2 ounces) Rolin brand "chilli bamboo shoots," drained

In a bowl, place the pork, salt, turmeric, and paprika. With your hands, mix the ingredients together thoroughly.

Heat the oil in a medium-sized saucepan over medium heat. Add the onion and sauté until translucent, about 5 minutes. Add the pork and stir continuously until the meat is browned, about 5 minutes. Add the water, cover, and simmer until the liquid is reduced to 1 cup, about 1 1/4 hours. Add the bamboo shoots and simmer, covered, until the liquid is reduced to 1/2 cup, about 10 minutes.

Serves 4.

Whetthar Thayetthee Thanut Hin
Pork Curry with Mango Pickle

Even though my mother is a great chef, she always gives credit to people who have given her a favorite recipe. She got this one from a Bengali cook. Homemade Bengali-style mango pickle is the best I've tasted, but commercial brands will have to do until green mangoes are more readily available in North American markets. I prefer Patak brand, which puts up a mild mango pickle.

2 pounds lean pork, cut into
    pieces 2 inches long and 1 inch wide
1 teaspoon salt
1 teaspoon ground turmeric
1 teaspoon fish sauce
3 tablespoons vegetable oil
1 yellow onion, finely chopped
1 tablespoon paprika
6 cups water
1/4 cup coarsely cut mango pickle

In a bowl, place the pork, salt, turmeric, and fish sauce. With your hands, mix the ingredients together thoroughly.

Heat the oil in a medium-sized saucepan over medium-low heat. Add the pork, onion, and paprika and sauté until the meat is nicely browned, about 5 minutes. Add the water, cover, and simmer until the liquid is reduced to 1 cup, about 1 1/4 hours. Add the mango pickle, reduce the heat to low, and cook uncovered, stirring frequently, until the liquid is reduced to 1/2 cup, about 10 minutes.

Serves 4.

Whetthar Pyoke Kyaw
Pork Roast Stew

I usually find roast pork rather dry. Although the Burmese put sauce on it, the sauce doesn't seem to penetrate the meat. Because of the cooking method used in this recipe, the pork is thoroughly moistened and the flavor of the meat is in harmony with the sauce—a new dish for people who love pork roast.

> 2 pounds boneless lean pork, cut into
>   2- by 1-inch pieces
> 3 tablespoons light soy sauce
> 2 tablespoons Worcestershire sauce
> 1/2 teaspoon ground black pepper
> 3 tablespoons vegetable oil
> 6 cups water
> 1 1/2 tablespoons cornstarch,
>   dissolved in 1/2 cup water

In a bowl, place the pork, soy sauce, Worcestershire sauce, and black pepper. With your hands, mix the ingredients together thoroughly and let stand for 30 minutes.

Heat the oil in a medium-sized saucepan over medium-low heat. Add the pork and sauté until the pork is browned, about 5 minutes. Add the water, cover, and simmer until the liquid is reduced to 1 cup, about 1 1/2 hours. (If the meat needs to cook longer, add a little water and continue to simmer until tender.)

Add the cornstarch mixture, stir thoroughly, and cook, uncovered, over medium-low heat until the pan juices thicken and coat the meat, about 10 minutes.

Serves 4.

Whethani Kyaw
Twice-Cooked Pork with Red Chile Pepper

The way to eat this dish is to add a little bit of it to a spoonful of steaming rice, and then add a dash of Split Mung Bean Soup (page 39) or any other soup of your choice.

1 1/2 pounds boneless lean pork butt or
    leg of pork, in one piece
1 tablespoon fish sauce
1/2 cup vegetable oil
2 medium-sized yellow onions, finely chopped
1 tablespoon chopped garlic
1 1/2 teaspoons crushed dried red chile pepper
1 1/2 teaspoons salt
1 teaspoon paprika

Place the pork in a saucepan and add water to cover. Bring to a boil, reduce the heat, and simmer until the pork is almost cooked through, about 30 minutes. Remove the pork from the pan and let cool to room temperature.

Cut the pork into strips measuring 1 inch long by 1/2 inch wide by 1/2 inch thick. Combine the pork strips and fish sauce in a bowl. With your hands, mix the ingredients together thoroughly and let stand for 10 minutes.

Heat the oil in a medium-sized frying pan over medium heat. Add the onions and fry until golden brown, about 6 minutes. Quickly add the garlic, chile, salt, paprika, and pork. Fry, stirring, until the pork is golden brown, about 8 minutes.

Serves 4.

Whetnanthar Kyaw
Fried Pork Chops

On my last painting trip in Burma before leaving for America, I went to the ancient city of Myohaung in the Arakan state, which is located in southwest Burma facing the Bay of Bengal. Although Myohaung was the center of the Arakanese kingdom eons ago, by the early seventies it had become a nondescript village with only one small food shop. From the three items that were available on the menu, my favorite was this pork chop served with simple boiled noodles. My main objective was to paint the landscape there, but after one whiff of his scrumptious dish, I took the time to write the recipe down in my diary. A dash of Worcestershire sauce (not in the original recipe) makes the dish tastier.

    2 medium-sized pork chops, about 3/4 inch thick
    2 egg yolks
    1 teaspoon finely chopped garlic
    1/4 teaspoon ground black pepper
    1 1/2 tablespoons light soy sauce
    1/2 tablespoon Worcestershire sauce
    1 tablespoon vegetable oil
    1 cup all-purpose flour

With a meat mallet or the blunt edge of a meat cleaver, pound the pork chops until they are about 1/2 inch thick. In a bowl, place the pork chops, egg yolks, garlic, pepper, soy sauce, and Worcestershire sauce. With your hands, mix the ingredients together thoroughly. Cover and refrigerate for 3 hours.

Heat the oil in a frying pan over medium heat. Dredge the chops in the flour and add to the pan. Fry gently, turning once, until golden brown on both sides, about 4 minutes per side.

Serves 2.

Whetnanyoe Paung
Steamed Ribs with Garlic

By cutting the ribs into small pieces, one can enjoy them freely without making a mess. In fact, the sauce makes the little ribs much juicier. They are excellent with steamed rice and any stir-fried vegetable dish.

> 3 pounds pork spareribs, in one slab
> 1 tablespoon finely minced garlic
> 1 tablespoon finely minced fresh ginger
> 1 teaspoon ground black pepper
> 1/2 teaspoon granulated sugar
> 6 tablespoons light soy sauce
> 1 tablespoon Asian sesame oil
> 1/4 teaspoon salt
> 1 1/2 teaspoons cornstarch, dissolved in 1/2 cup water

Have the butcher cut across the slab of spareribs to form 1 1/2-inch lengths, then cut the ribs apart.

In a bowl, combine all the ingredients except the cornstarch mixture. With your hands, mix the ingredients thoroughly and let stand for 3 hours in the refrigerator. Form a double thickness with 2 large sheets of aluminum foil. Bring all the sides up to form a boatlike shape and transfer the ribs and marinade to the foil "boat." Bring the foil edges together to form a loose package and seal securely. It is important that the juices not escape and that the steam does not get in. Pour water to a depth of about 2 inches in a steamer pan and bring to a boil. Place the foil package on the steamer rack, above the water, cover, and steam over gently boiling water for 1 hour. Unwrap the ribs and transfer them with their cooking juices to a frying pan over medium heat. Stir in the cornstarch mixture and cook until juices thicken, about 5 minutes.

Serves 4.

Whethar Kyamsaing Kyaw
Stir-Fried Pork with Preserved Mustard Leaves

There is a sizable population of ethnic Chinese who have lived in Burma for many generations. Among them are the Hakka Chinese, who most Asian scholars believe were a nomadic northern Chinese tribe who settled in the northeast corner of southern Guangdong province a thousand years ago. A dish like this that calls for preserved mustard certainly must have a Hakka origin, since most of the Burmese cottage industries that produce these greens are run by Hakkas. I have also noticed that when I serve my Hakka friends this dish, they eat it as if they were meeting a long-lost cousin.

1 pound boneless lean pork, cut into
   slices 1 inch long and 1/4 inch thick
1 tablespoon fish sauce
1/2 cup vegetable oil
1 yellow onion, finely chopped
3 garlic cloves, finely chopped
1 tablespoon julienned fresh ginger
1/2 cup diced celery
1/2 cup chopped green onion
2 cups preserved mustard greens, rinsed
   and cut into 1-inch cubes
1/2 teaspoon salt

In a bowl, place the pork and fish sauce. With your hands, mix the ingredients together thoroughly and let stand for 15 minutes.

Heat the oil in a 2-inch deep, medium-sized frying pan over medium-high heat. Add the yellow onion, garlic, and ginger and sauté until the onion begins to soften, 3 minutes. Add the pork, celery, green onion, and mustard. Cook, stirring, until the liquid evaporates and the pork is tender, about 8 minutes.

Serves 4.

Whetnanyoe Ghin
Barbecued Spareribs

At barbecues, potlucks, and picnics, I find that most Americans bring meat marinated in the same standard barbecue sauce, a practice that can produce a very monotonous meal. I always use this recipe as insurance that there will be some variety.

3 pounds pork spareribs, in one slab
2 teaspoons salt
2 teaspoons ground turmeric
5 tablespoons Worcestershire sauce
5 tablespoons light soy sauce
1 teaspoon ground black pepper

Using your hands, rub all the ingredients evenly on both sides of the spareribs. Cover and marinate for 3 hours in the refrigerator.

Prepare a fire in a charcoal grill. Cut the rib slab into single rib portions before cooking. Grill over medium-low coals, turning, until the meat is tender, about 30 minutes per side. Alternatively, arrange the ribs in a baking pan and bake in a preheated 350° F oven for 45 minutes.

Serves 4.

A few years ago, my mother became ill and I was called in to substitute for her on one of her catering jobs. I'd never before cooked meatloaf and it was the central dish among the others for which her client had asked. I was as nervous as hell. Thanks to the house butler, who gave me a double shot of brandy, I managed to produce this wonderful variation on a worldwide dish. From this experience, I also came to understand why cooks like to sip wine while cooking.

2 pounds ground pork
3 tablespoons ginger juice
1 tablespoon minced garlic
1 teaspoon ground black pepper
1/2 cup finely diced celery
3 tablespoons light soy sauce
1 teaspoon salt
3 whole eggs, plus 2 egg yolks

In a bowl, combine all the ingredients. With your hands, mix the ingredients together thoroughly and let stand for 1 hour.

Preheat the oven to 375° F. Line a 5- by 9-inch loaf pan with waxed paper. Fill the prepared pan with the pork mixture. Cover the pan tightly with aluminum foil and bake for 45 minutes. Alternatively, place the loaf pan on a rack in a steamer pan above about 2 inches of boiling water, cover, and steam for 1 hour.

Serves 4.

Whetchidauk Pyoke
Boiled Pig's Feet with Ginger and Garlic

The only time I've ever eaten pig's feet in public with any elegance was in Paris, where I ate pied de porc panné. *I shared this dish with friends who are passionate about pig's feet. But in America I have met many people who are quite squeamish about this delicacy.*

Buy the forefeet. They have more meat on them than the hind feet.

2 pig's forefeet
6 cloves garlic, crushed
6 medium-sized slices fresh ginger
1 teaspoon salt
1 tablespoon light soy sauce
3 quarts water
Garlic and Vinegar Sauce (page 21)

Ask the butcher to split the feet in half lengthwise and then cut each half crosswise into 4 pieces. Combine the pig's feet and all the remaining ingredients, except the sauce, in a large saucepan over medium heat. Cover and simmer until the pig's feet are tender, 2 to 2 1/2 hours.

Meanwhile, prepare the sauce and set aside. When the pig's feet are ready, serve with the sauce for dipping.

Serves 4.

For this dish I use stewing lamb, usually neck pieces and spareribs. No need to be extravagant and buy leg of lamb. I prefer the spareribs, although they demand extra work to remove the excess fat.

4 pounds lamb neck, cut into 1- to 2-inch pieces,
   or lamb spareribs, cut into 1 ¹/2-inch lengths and
   separated into individual ribs
1 ¹/2 teaspoons salt
1 ¹/2 teaspoons ground turmeric
1 tablespoon fish sauce
1 tablespoon paprika
2 tablespoons ground cumin
3 tablespoons vegetable oil
2 medium-sized yellow onions, finely chopped
2 tablespoons distilled white vinegar
6 cups water
2 medium-sized red potatoes, peeled and cut into eighths

Trim all visible fat from the neck pieces or spareribs. In a bowl, place the lamb, salt, turmeric, fish sauce, paprika, and cumin. With your hands, mix the ingredients together thoroughly.

Heat the oil in a medium-sized saucepan over medium-low heat. Add the onions and sauté until the onions begin to soften, 3 minutes. Add the lamb and vinegar, raise the heat to medium, and sauté until meat is browned, about 5 minutes. Add the water, cover, and simmer until the liquid is reduced to about 1 1/2 cups, about 1 1/4 hours. Add the potatoes, reduce the heat to low, and simmer until the potatoes are tender, about 20 minutes.

Serves 4.

Seikthar Ghin
Barbecued Leg of Lamb with Yogurt

Years ago two doctors from Burma visited me in San Francisco. They were both Muslims and wouldn't eat any meat if it wasn't halal, *or slaughtered according to Islamic law. I tried the "when in Rome" argument, but no dice. It was quite a headache. After many hours of anxious phoning, I finally found* halal *meat through a Muslim who was also from Burma, and I made the doctors this barbecue dish. They considered it a great treat.*

10 pounds leg of lamb, boned and cut into 1-inch cubes
2 1/2 cups plain yogurt
1 tablespoon salt
1 tablespoon ground turmeric
2 tablespoons paprika
1/4 cup ground cumin
1/2 teaspoon ground cloves
1/2 teaspoon ground nutmeg
5 tablespoons vegetable oil

In a large bowl, combine all the ingredients. With your hands, mix the ingredients together thoroughly. Cover and refrigerate overnight.

Prepare a fire in a charcoal grill. Thread the lamb cubes onto metal skewers and place over medium-hot coals. Grill until done to taste, about 7 minutes per side for medium.

Serves 12.

merican newspapers seldom carry stories about Burma. Now and then, however, I hear something about my homeland through the grapevine or from newly arrived immigrants. The first thing I always ask is the price of fish. That alone will tell the truth—what is really going on.

In recent years, the prices have gone sky-high. But I have been relieved to hear that inflation has only struck the prime fish and shellfish, such as shad, carp, halibut, lobster, and so on. They were expensive even when I was in Burma, although the costs had not reached such astronomical heights. Thanks to the many rivers, big and small, the average peasant family can still eat fish, although not the high-priced ones.

Sometimes I wonder whether the catfish was created just so that the poor would always have fish to eat. Catfish are abundant and can survive in almost any waters. They are a critical part of the diet in rural Burma.

During my early years in the United States, I couldn't quite understand why Americans, with their high standard of living, would go fishing. After all, there were so many markets where fish could be easily purchased. We Burmese find fishing for pleasure simply silly (not to mention the practice of sunbathing, which, to our way of thinking, is for people who cannot afford umbrellas). Fishing in Burma is for survival. I remember meeting people with their lines in the water along the Rangoon River even when the sun was already down. They would not go home empty-handed.

Shrimp, lobster, and crab are plentiful in Burmese waters, but not widely available in the market. The government-controlled fishing industries target these shellfish for export, to obtain much-needed foreign currency. That practice keeps the price high and the shellfish accessible to only the privileged class.

Zabalin Ngar Hin
Butterfish with Lemongrass

I was taught how to make this dish by a family who cared for me while I was on a painting trip in southeastern Burma. It was a beautiful, peaceful, and productive journey during which I tried to capture on canvas some of those magnificent surroundings. A little white stupa sat on a hill about a hundred yards from the family's home. Just before I left for America, they sent me a photograph of a lake with their village rooftops floating in the water. The white stupa stood in the background, spared by the nasty flood that had swept much of their community away. Whenever I eat this dish, I am transported back there alongside that stupa and I am at peace with the world around me.

1 tablespoon vegetable oil
2 pounds butterfish fillet (about 1 inch thick)
1 1/2 tablespoons distilled white vinegar
1 tablespoon thinly sliced fresh lemongrass
1 fresh jalepeño pepper, chopped
1/4 teaspoon salt
Pinch granulated sugar
1/2 cup water

Heat the oil in a frying pan over medium heat. Add the fish and then add all the remaining ingredients. Simmer gently, uncovered, until the fish is cooked, about 10 minutes, spooning the pan juices over the fish frequently.

Serves 4.

Ngathalok Kyaw
Fried Shad

Shad prepared in this manner is one of the most popular dishes in Burma's delta region. Glutinous rice cooked inside bamboo stalks is the favorite accompaniment.

One 3 pound shad, cleaned
$1/2$ teaspoon ground turmeric
1 teaspoon salt
2 cups vegetable oil

Cut the fish crosswise into 1-inch-thick steaks. Rub the steaks evenly with the turmeric and salt.

Heat the oil in a large frying pan over medium-high heat. Add the fish and fry, turning once, until golden brown, about 8 minutes per side. Do not worry if the steaks stick together as they cook; they can be separated when they are cool enough to handle. Remove the fish with a slotted utensil to paper towels to drain.

Serve warm or at room temperature.

Serves 4.

Ngapi Ye
Anchovy Sauce

Among Burmese, there is a saying: "If one hasn't eaten ngapi ye, one is not a true-blooded Burmese." Though I call it a sauce, it is actually a dish unto itself. One simply enjoys it together with any raw vegetable and steamed rice. In Burma, true ngapi ye is made from fermented dried fish, which many foreign noses find quite impolite. Some say it is worse than Limburger cheese. Kipling referred to it as "fish pickled when it ought to have been buried." With the availability of canned achovies in America, this dish can be made in a diplomatic manner. For those seeking a more authentic version, look for bottled fermented fish in any Asian market.

> 2 cans (1 3/4 ounces each) flat anchovy fillets in olive oil,
>   drained, or 4 ounces bottled fermented dried fish
> 1/2 cup water
> 1/4 cup shrimp powder
> 1 1/2 teaspoons crushed dried red chile pepper
> 1/4 cup freshly lemon juice
> 1 1/2 tablespoons finely minced garlic

Combine the fish and water in a small pan over medium heat. Bring to a boil and boil for 5 minutes, stirring and mashing the fish with a wooden spoon. Remove from the heat.

In a small bowl, combine the mashed fish with all the remaining ingredients and mix well.

Serves 4.

Balachung
Shredded Dried Shrimp Condiment

Like ngapi ye, *the anchovy dip,* balachung *(which is also called* pazunchauk ngapi gyaw) *is widely eaten as a condiment with meals. Or it is simply eaten alone with plain steamed rice. When a Burmese family travels, a container of* balachung *is always at hand. Stored in a closed jar at room temperature, it will keep for three months. Spread it on toast to make delicious sandwiches.*

1 cup dried shrimp
1 yellow onion
1 cup vegetable oil
$^1/_2$ teaspoon ground turmeric
8 cloves garlic, thinly sliced
1 teaspoon paprika
$^1/_2$ teaspoon salt
2 tablespoons crushed dried red chile pepper
2 tablespoons distilled white vinegar
2 teaspoons granulated sugar

Shred the dried shrimp in a blender and set aside. Cut the onion in half vertically and then slice the halves thinly to form crescent-shaped fans.

Heat the oil in a frying pan over medium heat. Add onion and turmeric and cook until the onion begins to color, about 3 minutes. Add the garlic and continue to cook until the onion and garlic are golden brown, about 6 minutes.

Add the shredded shrimp, paprika, salt, chile pepper, vinegar, and sugar and stir-fry for 3 minutes.

Remove from the heat and let cool to room temperature before serving. Save the leftovers in a closed jar.

Serves 6.

I find pompano rich and a bit saltier than many other fish. Eaten in small amounts with steamed rice, it creates a perfect balance of flavors. Bottleneck Gourd Soup (page 40) complements this dish.

One 1-pound pompano, cleaned
2 tablespoons light soy sauce
1/4 teaspoon ground turmeric
3 tablespoons vegetable oil
1 tablespoon water
1 yellow onion, sliced into 1/2-inch-thick rings

With a sharp knife, make 3 slashes 1/8 inch deep and 1 inch apart on both sides of the fish and place in a shallow bowl. Rub the fish evenly with the soy sauce and turmeric. Let stand for 10 minutes.

Heat the oil in a large frying pan over medium heat. Add the fish and its marinade and fry for 1 minute. Sprinkle the water over the fish and continue to cook for 3 minutes.

Remove the pan from the burner and let stand for 1 minute. With a wide spatula, gently turn the fish. Return the pan to medium heat and add the onion rings. Cook until the fish and onions are tender, 10 minutes.

Serves 4.

Kakuyan Ngar Kyaw
Fried Kingfish

This dish is a good counterpoint to a meat curry. The sweet, mild taste of the fish goes well with a complex curry sauce.

Four 7-inch kingfish, cleaned
1/2 teaspoon salt
1/2 teaspoon ground turmeric
1 cup vegetable oil

With a sharp knife, make 3 slashes 1/8 inch deep and 1 inch apart on both sides of the fish. Rub the fish evenly with the salt and turmeric.

Heat the oil in a large frying pan over medium heat. Slip the fish into the pan and fry, turning once, until golden brown on both sides, 3 to 4 minutes per side.

Serves 4.

Kakuyan Ngar Hin
Kingfish Curry

Although the kingfish is small, it is one of the best fish to cook in the curry style. It is inexpensive in Burma and mostly eaten by the poor. It is also inexpensive in the United States. Yet, as with many peasant foods, it is extremely flavorful. Brought up with an abundance of food on the table, I was startled on my first trip into the countryside to find myself sharing a meager meal of kingfish and rice with six members of a villager's family. The simple fare turned out to be a delight, and everyone smiled and rejoiced at the honor of hosting a city man at their humble country table. It was a lesson in the art of sharing I will never forget.

> Four 7-inch kingfish, cleaned and heads removed
> 1 teaspoon salt
> 1/2 teaspoon ground turmeric
> 1/4 cup vegetable oil
> 1 yellow onion, finely chopped
> 1 medium-sized tomato, cut into eighths
> 1 teaspoon paprika
> 1 tablespoon ground cumin
> 1 tablespoon finely chopped fresh cilantro
> 2 tablespoons fresh lemon juice
> 1/2 cup water

With a sharp knife, make 3 slashes 1/8 inch deep and 1 inch apart on both sides of the fish. Rub the fish evenly with the salt and turmeric, set aside.

Heat the oil in a large, 2-inch-deep frying pan over medium heat. Add the onion and tomatoes and sauté until the tomatoes are soft, about 5 minutes. Add the paprika, cumin, cilantro, and 1 tablespoon of the lemon juice and cook for 5 minutes, stirring frequently. Add the fish and water and spoon the pan juices over the fish. Cover and simmer for 3 minutes. Uncover the pan, turn the fish over, and simmer until the fish are done, 5 minutes. Sprinkle the remaining 1 tablespoon lemon juice over the top.

Serves 4.

People who like piquant food will find this dish especially appealing. It goes extremely well with Yellow Split Pea Soup (page 42) and steamed rice.

5 snapper steaks (about 2 inches thick)
1/2 teaspoon ground turmeric
1 1/2 teaspoons salt
1 cup plus 2 tablespoons vegetable oil
1 large yellow onion
4 cloves garlic, chopped
1 tablespoon crushed dried red chile pepper, or to taste
1/2 cup finely sliced green onion

Rub the fish steaks evenly with the turmeric and salt. Heat the 1 1/2 cups oil in a large frying pan over medium-high heat. Slip the steaks into the pan and fry, turning once, until golden brown on both sides, about 10 minutes per side. Remove the fish from the pan, reserving the oil in the pan, and set aside.

Cut the yellow onion in half vertically and then slice thinly to form crescent-shaped fans. Heat the reserved oil in the pan over medium heat. Add the onion and sauté until golden brown, about 6 minutes. Drain the onion and set aside.

In another large frying pan, heat the 2 tablespoons oil over medium heat. Add the garlic and sauté until it begins to turn brown. Add the chile and cook, stirring, for 30 seconds. Add the reserved fish and fried onion and stir gently to mix. Transfer to a serving plate and garnish with green onion.

Serves 4.

Ngar Pei-Ngun-Pyar-Ye
Sole with Soy Sauce

Although this is the quickest and easiest way to cook sole, it results in a fanciful flavor. It is a perfect dish for two or four when you don't feel like spending a lot of time in the kitchen. Prepare it just before you plan to serve it.

1 1/2 teaspoons vegetable oil
One 2-pound sole, cleaned and head removed
1 1/2 teaspoons chopped garlic
3 tablespoons light soy sauce
1 teaspoon Asian sesame oil
1/2 teaspoon finely minced fresh ginger
1/2 cup water
3 green onions, finely chopped

Heat the vegetable oil in a large frying pan over medium heat. Slip the fish into the pan, light side down, and fry for 5 minutes. Remove the pan from the burner and let stand for 2 minutes. With a wide spatula, gently turn the fish over. Return the pan to medium-high heat and add the garlic, soy sauce, sesame oil, ginger, and water. Cover and cook for 5 minutes. Uncover and cook until the fish is done, about 5 minutes.

Transfer to a serving plate and garnish with the green onions.

Serves 4.

Masala Ngar Hin
Sea Bass Curry with Cumin

You'll be surprised how the smell of the sea and the spicy fragrance of cumin comingle for a savory aroma. This recipe is also possible with any firm fish, such as cod, haddock, or monkfish.

> 5 sea bass steaks (about 2 inches thick)
> 1/2 teaspoon ground turmeric
> 1 1/2 teaspoons salt
> 1/4 cup vegetable oil
> 1 yellow onion, finely chopped
> 1 teaspoon paprika
> 1/2 teaspoon ground cayenne pepper
> 1/2 cup tamarind juice
> 1 cup water
> 3 tablespoons ground cumin

Rub the fish steaks evenly with the turmeric and salt; set aside.

Heat the oil in a large, 2-inch-deep frying pan over medium heat. Add the onion, paprika, and cayenne and sauté until the onion is translucent, about 5 minutes.

Add the tamarind juice and water. Cover and simmer until the liquid is reduced by three quarters. Add the fish and cumin and simmer, uncovered, turning once, until the fish is cooked, about 10 minutes per side.

Serves 4.

Ngarpaung Toke
Fish in Banana Leaves

In Burma whenever there was a special occasion that called for our best, this dish was at the top of the family menu. It was a dish developed by my mother and often used when foreign dignitaries visited our home. The aroma of the banana leaf crowns the fish like a jewel.

2 pounds firm fish fillet, such as cod or snapper
1 teaspoon finely minced garlic
1/2 cup finely chopped onion
1 1/2 teaspoons ground lemongrass
1 teaspoon paprika
1/4 teaspoon ground cayenne pepper
2 teaspoons salt
1 tablespoon ginger juice
3 tablespoons vegetable oil
1 tablespoon cornstarch
3 tablespoons grated dried coconut
Eight 8-inch-square pieces banana leaf

Cut the fish into 2 1/2-inch squares about 1/2 inch thick. In a bowl, place the fish and all the remaining ingredients except the banana leaves. With your hands, mix the ingredients together thoroughly.

Dip banana leaves in hot water for 15 seconds, or until soft. Divide the fish mixture evenly among the 8 banana-leaf squares, arranging the pieces in the center. Fold in the sides of each square to form an envelope shape and secure in place with 1 or more toothpicks.

Pour water to a depth of 2 inches into a steamer pan and bring to a boil. Place the packets on the steamed rack above gently boiling water, cover, and steam for 30 minutes.

Serves 6 to 8.

Ngathalok Paung
Steamed Shad in a Pressure Cooker

Hilsa is the most prized fish in Burma. In America we Burmese are happy to have shad, since it's like the hilsa's twin brother. Many people have eaten shad roe, but only a few have discovered shad. Probably the pinbones keep folks away from it. But if you are careful, this fish can become a favorite. This recipe calls for a pressure cooker, so the bones will pose no problem.

    One 3-pound shad, cleaned
    1 tablespoon pressed garlic
    1 tablespoon ginger juice
    1 teaspoon salt
    1 tablespoon light soy sauce
    1/4 teaspoon granulated sugar
    1/4 teaspoon ground black pepper

Place the fish in a shallow dish and rub it evenly with all the remaining ingredients. Let stand for 1 to 2 hours.

If the fish will not fit in your pressure cooker, cut off the head and tail or cut the fish in half crosswise. Place the fish on a large sheet of aluminum foil; fold in the sides, and seal in the fish securely. Pour water to a depth of 2 inches into the bottom of the pressure cooker. Place the fish on the pressure cooker rack, cover, and cook the fish at medium pressure for 30 minutes.

Serves 4.

I had a discussion once with a group of Western friends about various sorts of cutlets and how they differ from the Burmese kind. I'd say mine is more piquant than all other versions I've eaten. The Burmese adopted the idea of making cutlets from the British, but the taste of this dish is definitely Burmese.

> 2 pounds firm fish fillet, such as cod or snapper
> 1 1/2 cups mashed cooked potato
> 1/2 cup finely sliced green onion
> 1 tablespoon salt
> 2 egg yolks, beaten
> 1 teaspoon minced garlic
> 1/2 teaspoon Tabasco sauce
> 1/2 teaspoon ground black pepper
> 1/2 cup vegetable oil
> All-purpose flour for dusting

Fill a wide-bottomed saucepan or a deep skillet with enough water to immerse the fish fillet completely. Bring to a boil and add the fish. Boil gently until the fish flakes when pierced with a fork, about 5 minutes. Remove the fish and let cool to room temperature.

In a large bowl, break up the fish. Add all the remaining ingredients except the oil and flour and, with your hands, mix to distribute the ingredients evenly. Form the mixture into 6 patties, 1 inch thick.

Heat the oil in a large frying pan over medium heat. Dust the patties with flour and slip them into the hot oil. Fry, turning once, until golden brown on both sides, about 2 minutes per side.

Serves 4.

Ngaphelone Hin
Ladyfish Ball Curry

Chinese cooks use ladyfish paste to make fish balls for serving in soup, for stir-frying with greens, or for stuffing bean curd. Here the same fish paste is used to make balls for a Burmese curry. Ladyfish paste can be found in Chinese fish markets.

> Vegetable oil for rubbing on hands,
>   plus 3 tablespoons vegetable oil for sautéing
> 2 pounds ladyfish paste
> 1 yellow onion, chopped
> 1 teaspoon finely minced fresh ginger
> 1 teaspoon ground turmeric
> 1/2 teaspoon salt
> 1/2 cup diced (1/4 inch) tomato
> 1/2 cup water

Rub a generous amount of oil on both hands to reduce the stickiness of working with the fish paste. Form the fish paste into bite-sized balls; set aside.

Heat the 3 tablespoons oil in a medium-sized saucepan over medium heat. Add the onion, ginger, turmeric, salt, and tomato and sauté until the tomato becomes soft and begins to fall apart. Add 1 or 2 spoonfuls of water if the mixture becomes too dry before the tomato softens. Add the fish balls and water and simmer uncovered, stirring occasionally, until the liquid is reduced by half and the fish balls are cooked, about 10 minutes.

Serves 4.

Ngartitar Hin
Canned Tuna with Lemongrass

This is perhaps the most popular dish I have developed in America. In the first months after my arrival I was very homesick. I didn't venture out much and was unaware of the supermarkets and shopping areas around town. Across the street from my apartment stood a grocery store called Lem's Market, owned by a very charming but reticent Chinese family. There I discovered my first can of tuna. Out of many attempts to create something with canned fish, this recipe was the most outstanding. It resembles a native Burmese dish called ngabutmwe.

> 4 teaspoons vegetable oil
> 1 yellow onion, finely minced
> 1/2 teaspoon ground turmeric
> 1 teaspoon chopped garlic
> 1/2 teaspoon paprika
> 1 stalk fresh lemongrass, trimmed and finely sliced
> 2 cans (16 1/8 ounces each) tuna packed in
>   water, well drained
> 1 teaspoon salt
> 1/2 cup water

Heat the oil in a medium-sized saucepan over medium heat. Add the onion, turmeric, garlic, paprika, and lemongrass and sauté until the onion begins to soften, 3 minutes.

Add the tuna and salt. Stir for 1 minute and add the water. Simmer uncovered for 10 minutes.

Serves 4.

When my father came to the States for the first time, I hadn't seen him in eighteen years. While we reminisced I realized that I had completely forgotten this dish. It comes from the city of Moulmein, where he was born.

 2 pounds firm fish fillet, such as snapper or cod
 1 tablespoon finely minced fresh ginger
 1 tablespoon finely chopped garlic
 1 tablespoon thinly sliced fresh lemongrass
 2 teaspoons salt
 1 teaspoon ground turmeric
 1 1/2 tablespoons partially ground mild green chile pepper
 2 egg yolks, beaten
 1/2 cup all-purpose flour
 2 cups vegetable oil for frying

Cut the fillet into pieces 2 inches long and 5/8 inch wide. In a bowl, place the fish and all the remaining ingredients except the oil. With your hands, mix the ingredients together thoroughly. Form the fish mixture into bite-sized patties.

Heat the oil in a large, 2-inch-deep frying pan over medium-high heat. Slip the patties into the oil and fry, turning once, until golden brown on both sides, about 4 minutes per side.

Serves 4.

Nananpin Ngakhu Hin
Catfish Curry with Tomato and Cilantro

Most Asians prefer to cook freshly killed catfish. They say it tastes better. As evidence of this, one can see tanks full of live catfish at Asian fish markets and restaurants. Readers who wish to prepare this dish are advised to go to an Asian market for the freshest fish. But I have the duty of describing the scenario of that visit so that you can decide whether to buy a dead or a live catfish.

I would definitely pick a freshly killed fish displayed on crushed ice. Why? For the simple reason that I find it unpleasant witnessing a fish being knocked on the head with a mallet and still deprived of sudden death. The catfish will flutter and wiggle in the plastic bag on their way to your kitchen. No doubt my squeamishness can be easily challenged by a forensic pathologist who might say killing this way is humane because brain laceration prevents all conscious pain and death follows soon after, and that the fluttering and the wiggling are nothing but reflex actions. But humaneness rests in the eye of the shopper, not in the eye of the victim, and what we see is a brutal and gruesome act.

I know it's ridiculous to be contemplating this issue while writing a recipe for catfish. And, as long as people want meat on their tables, killing is inevitable. But there is an important difference between the killing of animals for food and the process of brutality involved in satisfying the fantasy of the overrefined gourmet. I protest skinning the snake alive, forcing the duck to dance on a hot plate, boxing the calf for veal, smothering the pigeon, and so on. They are odious acts of deception, committed in the name of freshness.

If you must have the catfish freshly killed, I would exhort you to ask the fishmonger behind the counter to hack off its head with the cleaver. Boom, no theater. And if he says, "Ah ... no, no, lose weight, less money," then tell him you will pay for the head. There are so many fresh fish, including catfish, available at fish markets with no apparent head injuries. Let's buy them.

Even though catfish look dark and nasty, they have a sweet and mellow taste. Beauty is skin deep, as they say. Anyway, this is a wonderful recipe my family has been enjoying for many, many years. Bon appétit!

One 3-pound catfish, cleaned and head removed
1/2 teaspoon ground turmeric
1/2 teaspoon salt
1/4 cup vegetable oil
1 yellow onion, finely chopped
3 cloves garlic, finely minced
1 teaspoon paprika
1 cup chopped tomato
8 sprigs fresh cilantro

Cut the fins off the fish and remove the slimy film that covers the skin with a knife or scrub it away with a vegetable brush. Beginning at the head end, cut the catfish into 1-inch-thick steaks. Rub the fish steaks evenly with the turmeric and salt. Let stand for 30 minutes.

Heat the oil in a large, 3-inch-deep frying pan over medium heat. Add the onion, garlic, paprika, and tomato and sauté until the onion is translucent, about 5 minutes. Add the water, cover, and simmer until liquid is reduced by three quarters, about 20 minutes.

Lay the fish steaks flat in the pan; do not overlap the steaks if possible. Spoon the pan juices over the fish. Cover, and cook until the fish is done, about 10 minutes. Turn off the heat, sprinkle with the cilantro, and let stand, covered, for about 15 minutes before serving.

Serves 4.

When I was in Gainesville, Florida, the first thing I saw that made me homesick was a roadside shop selling fried catfish. Catfish is the most popular fish in Burma and can be found abundantly in all of the country's many rivers. I have happy memories of fishing trips along the Irrawaddy, when I would join with the village boys in a mad battle to catch the most fish. Though it was recreational for me, it was a matter of catching dinner for my comrades.

Frying catfish is common in all Burmese households, where the fish is often eaten with steamed rice and Water Spinach Soup (page 38). At Asian fish markets you will find different sizes of catfish. The six- to eight-inch fish are the best ones for this dish.

Six 6- to 8-inch catfish, cleaned
1 teaspoon ground turmeric
1 1/2 teaspoons salt
3 cups vegetable oil

Cut the fins off the fish and remove the slimy film that covers the skin with a knife or scrub it away with a vegetable brush. Using a sharp knife, make 3 slashes 1/8 inch deep and 1 inch apart on both sides of each fish. Rub the fish evenly with the turmeric and salt. Let stand for 30 minutes.

Heat the oil in a large, 2-inch-deep frying pan over high heat. Slip the fish into the skillet and fry until golden brown on the first side, about 8 minutes. Turn the fish over and fry on the second side until golden brown, about 6 minutes longer.

Serves 4.

About Shrimp Curry

Whenever we requested shrimp curry in our household in Rangoon, the cook always asked specifically which particular taste we desired: sweet, sour, hot and spicy, or bitter. He would use potatoes and bottleneck gourd for sweet curry, chinbaung *leaves for sour, cumin and ground cayenne for hot and spicy, and bitter melon for bitter. The following four recipes, in order, reflect these tastes. Since* chinbaung, *a popular vegetable in Burma, is unavailable in America, I have had to use rhubarb, which is a fine substitute. All of these curries should be prepared with headless medium-sized shrimp.*

1 1/2 pounds headless medium-sized shrimp,
   peeled and deveined
1/2 teaspoon ground turmeric
1 1/2 teaspoons salt
1/4 cup vegetable oil
1 yellow onion, finely chopped
1 teaspoon paprika
2 medium-sized red potatoes, peeled and
   cut into quarters
1 cup water

In a bowl, place the shrimp, turmeric, and salt. With your hands, mix the ingredients together thoroughly and set aside.

Heat the oil in a medium-sized saucepan over medium heat. Add the onion and sauté until translucent, about 5 minutes. Add the paprika, potatoes, and water; cover and simmer until potatoes are tender, 20 to 25 minutes. Add the shrimp and simmer, uncovered, until the shrimp are cooked, about 5 minutes.

Serves 4.

Pazun Buthee Hin
Shrimp Curry with Bottleneck Gourd

1 1/2 pounds headless medium-sized shrimp,
   peeled and deveined
1 pound bottleneck gourds
1/2 teaspoon ground turmeric
1 1/2 teaspoons salt
1/4 cup vegetable oil
1 yellow onion, finely chopped
1 teaspoon paprika
1 teaspoon pressed garlic
1/2 teaspoon finely chopped fresh ginger
1/2 teaspoon fish sauce
1/2 cup water

In a bowl, place the shrimp, turmeric, and salt. With your hands, mix the ingredients together thoroughly and set aside. Peel the gourd. Cut in half lengthwise and scrape out and discard the seeds and pith. Cut the gourd into 1 1/2-inch cubes; set aside.

Heat the oil in a medium-sized saucepan over medium heat. Add the onion, paprika, garlic, and ginger and sauté until the onion begins to soften, 3 minutes. Add the fish sauce, gourd, and water. Cover and simmer, stirring frequently but gently, until the gourd pieces are translucent, about 8 minutes. Add the shrimp and simmer, covered, until the shrimp are cooked, about 5 minutes.

Serves 4.

Pazun Chinbaung Hin
Shrimp Curry with Rhubarb

1 1/2 pounds headless medium-sized shrimp,
  peeled and deveined
1/2 teaspoon ground turmeric
1 1/2 teaspoons salt
1 yellow onion, finely chopped
1 teaspoon paprika
1/2 teaspoon fish sauce
2 rhubarb stalks, peeled of all fibrous threads and
  cut into 2-inch lengths
2 cups spinach leaves
5 tablespoons vegetable oil
1/2 cup water

In a bowl, place the shrimp, turmeric, and salt. With your hands, mix the ingredients thoroughly; set aside.

In a medium-sized saucepan over medium heat, place the onion, paprika, fish sauce, rhubarb, spinach, oil, and water. Cover and cook, stirring frequently, until the rhubarb and spinach are tender, about 10 minutes. Add the shrimp and simmer, covered, until the shrimp are cooked, about 5 minutes.

Serves 4.

Pazun Masala Hin
Shrimp Curry with Cumin

2 pounds headless medium-sized shrimp,
  peeled and deveined
$^1/_2$ teaspoon ground turmeric
$^1/_2$ teaspoon salt
5 tablespoons vegetable oil
1 yellow onion, finely chopped
1 teaspoon paprika
$^1/_2$ teaspoon fish sauce
$^1/_2$ cup water
2 tablespoons ground cumin
3 fresh sprigs cilantro

In a bowl, place the shrimp, turmeric, and salt. With your hands, mix the ingredients together thoroughly and set aside.

Heat the oil in a medium-sized saucepan over medium heat. Add the onion and sauté until it begins to soften, about 3 minutes. Add the paprika, fish sauce, and water. Simmer until the liquid is reduced by half, about 5 minutes. Add the cumin, shrimp, and cilantro and simmer uncovered, stirring frequently, until the shrimp are cooked, about 5 minutes.

Serves 4.

Garnun Hin
Crab Curry

Back in Rangoon, this curry was served every Sunday for lunch. It was my father's favorite meal, and I sometimes wonder what he would have done if it had not shown up on the table.

Today, except for my father, who decided to remain in Burma, my family resides in America. My sister's husband and my girlfriend are Americans. When we get together for Christmas we honor both sides with a turkey on Christmas Eve and this curry on Christmas Day. I must admit, though, this seems to be the more eagerly awaited of the two meals.

> Two 3-pound live Dungeness crabs
> 1 cup vegetable oil
> 2 yellow onions, finely chopped
> 1 tablespoon minced garlic
> 1 tablespoon chopped fresh ginger
> 1 teaspoon ground turmeric
> 1/2 cup ground cumin
> 1 1/2 tablespoons salt
> 1 1/2 teaspoons ground cardamom
> 1 tablespoon ground coriander
> 1 1/2 teaspoons fenugreek
> 2 bay leaves
> 1 tablespoon paprika
> 1/2 cup distilled white vinegar

Pour water to a depth of 1 inch into a large pot. Bring the water to a boil, add the crabs, cover, and cook for 7 minutes. (If you are faint of heart, leave the kitchen for the 7 minutes.) Remove the crabs from the pot and let them cool completely.

Remove the claws and legs from the crab bodies. Pull the entire chest section from the carapace, or hard shell. Pull off and discard the gills, which are the feathery spongy strips. Cut the chest section into 4 pieces. Scrape out and collect the tomalley, the creamy substance in the chest cavity, from the carapaces. (Reserve the carapaces to use for making Baked Stuffed Crab (following recipe).

Heat the oil in a large, wide-bottomed pan over medium heat. Add all the remaining ingredients, including the tomalley but not the crab pieces, and sauté until the onions begin to soften, about 3 minutes. Add the crab pieces, mix thoroughly, cover, and simmer for 10 minutes. Uncover and simmer, stirring, for 10 minutes longer.

Serves 2.

Garnun Paung

Stuffed Baked Crab

Crabs are commonly found in the brackish waters of southern Burma's vast delta area, so Burmese eat crab all year around. In America, crabs are rather expensive, even in season. This dish is a perfect follow-up to the preceding recipe for Crab Curry, since you can put the saved shells to use.

> 1 pound crab meat, picked over to
>   remove any shell fragments
> 1 yellow onion, finely chopped
> 1 can (16 1/8 ounces) whole bamboo shoots,
>   drained and chopped
> 1 can (6 1/8 ounces) water chestnuts,
>   drained and chopped
> 1 1/2 teaspoons salt
> 2 green onions, thinly sliced
> 1 tablespoon light soy sauce
> 2 egg yolks
> 1/2 teaspoon ground black pepper
> 2 tablespoons butter
> 1 tablespoon all-purpose flour
> 2 crab shells saved from Crab Curry (preceding recipe)

Preheat the oven to 350° F. In a bowl, place all the ingredients except the crab shells. With your hands, mix the ingredients together thoroughly.

Stuff the crab mixture into the shells and place the shells in a shallow baking dish, stuffing side up. Bake for 30 minutes.

Serve the crab mixture in the shell.

Serves 2.

U nless the world's weather patterns change, the Burmese people will not starve. Because of its tropical rains, Burma has a plethora of vegetables and fruits. And, in spite of the meat, fish, and shellfish dishes we have with our meals, the love of vegetables is intense and indispensable to Burmese cuisine.

According to the Burmese way of eating, salads are part of the main meal, served alongside the curries and other dishes. They are also eaten as snacks or as a single dish at lunchtime. Salads are made from greens, vegetables, or even fruits. Young jackfruit, green mangoes, and baby eggplants, either raw or blanched, are served along with *ngapi ye*, our anchovy sauce, for dipping. A typical Burmese meal must have at least two kinds of salad (greens, vegetables, or fruits) and a bowl of *ngapi ye*. We can gladly do without meat or fish dishes if we must.

A tangy alternative to American coleslaw.

1/4 cup chana dal powder
One 2-pound green cabbage
1 yellow onion
1/4 teaspoon ground turmeric
1/2 cup vegetable oil
1/4 cup fresh lemon juice
1 1/2 teaspoons salt, or to taste
1/2 cup thinly sliced green onion

Heat a small, dry frying pan over medium heat. Add the chana dal powder and stir constantly until light brown, about 4 minutes; set aside.

Remove any outer bruised leaves of the cabbage. Cut the cabbage in half vertically and cut out the hard core. Thinly slice the cabbage, but not so thinly that it is shredded; set aside in a large bowl.

Cut the onion in half vertically and then slice the halves thinly to form crescent-shaped fans. Heat the oil in a skillet over medium heat. Add the onion and turmeric and saute until golden brown, about 6 minutes. Drain the onion, reserving 3 tablespoons of the oil, and set the onion and oil aside.

Add the lemon juice, toasted dal powder, salt, green onion, and onion and oil to the cabbage. Mix well.

Serves 4.

Ngayokese Kyethunchin
Onion with Sriracha Chile Sauce

Sriracha chile sauce is very versatile—the Southeast Asian answer to ketchup. It is widely used in Burma as a condiment with fried rice or noodles and makes an excellent dressing for sliced onions.

    5 tablespoons Sriracha chile sauce
    1 yellow onion

Cut the onion in half vertically and then slice thinly to form crescent-shaped fans. In a bowl, combine the chili sauce and onion and mix well.

Serves 4.

Thakwarthee Kyethun Chin
Cucumber-Onion Salad

This, the most basic salad in Burmese cuisine, goes well with almost any curry dish. It is very easy to make, and it is best when assembled just before serving.

2 large cucumbers
1 yellow onion
1 tablespoon distilled white vinegar
1 tablespoon fresh lemon juice
1 1/2 teaspoons salt

Peel the cucumbers and cut them in half lengthwise. Scrape out and discard the seeds and cut the cucumbers into 1/4-inch-thick slices. Place in a large bowl. Cut the onion in half vertically and then slice the halves thinly to form crescent-shaped fans. Add the onion to the cucumber.

Add the vinegar, lemon juice, and salt; mix well. Serve immediately.

Serves 4.

Tharkwarthee Dainchin
Cucumber Salad with Buttermilk

A soothing salad that goes hand in hand with hot, spicy curries. The Burmese learned the value of buttermilk as a coolant for hot weather and spicy food. This dish is an especially good counterpoint to curries that contain cumin.

2 cucumbers
1 1/2 cups buttermilk
1/4 teaspoon ground black pepper
1 tablespoon finely chopped fresh parsley

Peel the cucumbers and cut them in half lengthwise. Scrape out and discard the seeds. Cut the cucumber into 1/4-inch-thick slices.

In a bowl, combine all the ingredients and mix well.

Serves 4.

Pashoe Thanut

Cucumber Salad with Sesame Seed

I have never seen or served this dish at any household other than my own. It is a premier salad and an excellent accompaniment to a formal dinner. People always ask, "How do you make these cucumbers so crunchy?" Here's the secret.

4 cucumbers
1/4 cup julienned fresh ginger
1/2 cup distilled white vinegar
1/4 cup granulated sugar
3 tablespoons salt, plus salt to taste
1 large yellow onion
1 cup vegetable oil
1/4 teaspoon ground turmeric
1/4 cup sesame seed
1/4 cup shrimp powder

Peel the cucumbers and cut in half lengthwise. Scrape out and discard the seeds. Slice the cucumbers very thinly. Place the cucumber slices in a bowl and add the ginger, vinegar, sugar, and the 3 tablespoons salt. Mix well. Marinate for 2 hours. Transfer the cucumber slices to the center of a piece of cheesecloth. Gather up the corners of the cloth and twist together to enclose the cucumber slices securely. Squeeze out as much liquid as possible. Set the cheesecloth package on a flat surface and top with a heavy weight. Let stand for 1 hour.

Meanwhile, cut the onion in half vertically and then slice the halves thinly to form crescent-shaped fans. Heat the oil in a skillet over medium heat. Add the onion and turmeric and sauté until golden brown, about 6 minutes. Drain the onion, reserving 1 1/2 tablespoons of the oil, and set the onion and oil aside.

Heat a small, dry frying pan over medium heat. Add the sesame seed and stir constantly until the seeds are light brown and begin to pop, about 3 minutes.

Unwrap the cucumber slices and place them in a large bowl. Add the onion and oil, sesame seed, and shrimp powder. Mix well and add salt to taste. Serves 4.

Peitheeshay Pashoe Thanut
Asian Long Bean Salad

For an exquisite Burmese banquet, we usually serve this dish in a bowl next to a bowl of Cucumber Salad (page 148), or we put the two salads alongside each other on a platter. The long beans can be easily found in any Asian produce market.

1 teaspoon baking soda
1 pound long beans
1 large yellow onion
1 cup vegetable oil
1/4 teaspoon ground turmeric
3 tablespoons sesame seed
1/4 cup shrimp powder
1 1/2 teaspoons salt

Fill a large saucepan with water and bring to a boil. Add the baking soda and the beans and blanch for 1 1/2 minutes. Drain and cool to room temperature, then cut into 1/4-inch-thick pieces. Set aside.

Cut the onion in half vertically and then slice the halves thinly to form crescent-shaped fans. Heat the oil in a frying pan over medium heat. Add the onion and turmeric and sauté until golden brown, about 6 minutes. Drain the onion, reserving 2 tablespoons of the oil, and set the onion and oil aside.

Heat a small, dry frying pan over medium heat. Add the sesame seed and stir constantly until the seeds are light brown and begin to pop, 3 to 4 minutes.

In a bowl, combine the beans, onion and oil, toasted sesame seed, shrimp powder, and salt. Mix well.

Serves 4.

Khayanchinthee Thoke
Tomato Salad

Vine-ripened tomatoes should be used for preparing this salad. Any tomato will do in a pinch, however. This is a refreshing side dish with most meat curries.

1 large yellow onion
1 cup vegetable oil
1/4 teaspoon ground turmeric
1/4 cup chana dal powder
6 medium-sized tomatoes
1/2 cup thinly chopped green onion
3 tablespoons fresh lime juice
1/4 cup shrimp powder
1/2 cup roasted and skinned peanuts,
    finely ground in a blender or nut grinder
1/2 teaspoon salt, or to taste

Cut the yellow onion in half vertically and then slice the halves thinly to form crescent-shaped fans. Heat the oil in a frying pan over medium heat. Add the onion and turmeric and sauté until golden brown, about 6 minutes. Drain the onion, reserving 3 tablespoons of the oil, and set the onion and oil aside.

Heat a small, dry frying pan over medium heat. Add the chana dal powder and stir constantly until light brown, about 4 minutes; set aside.

Cut the tomatoes in half vertically. Scoop out and discard the seeds and cut the tomatoes into 1/4-inch-thick slices. Place the tomato slices in a large bowl, add the onion and oil, chana dal powder, and all the remaining ingredients. Mix well.

Serves 4.

Myinsharpei Thoke
Garbanzo Bean Salad

Before the military government banned horse racing, Burmese horse trainers believed feeding garbanzo beans to their charges made them healthier and faster runners. Joggers might like to try this salad, but I prefer it as a TV snack.

1 yellow onion
2 cans (16 ounces) garbanzo beans, well drained
3 cloves garlic, thinly sliced
1/4 cup vegetable oil
1 teaspoon salt
1 tablespoon finely chopped fresh cilantro

Cut the onion in half vertically and then slice thinly to form crescent-shaped fans.

In a large bowl, combine the onion and all the remaining ingredients. Mix well.

Serves 4.

Monlar On Achin
Daikon Salad

When I was finishing my Burmese memoir, Visions of Shwedagon *at a farm in Minnesota, I took along the Asian spices that were hard to find in that part of the country. I also carried some daikon seeds because I had been told that this popular Asian root vegetable did not exist in middle America. I became over enthusiastic and seeded about twelve rows of daikon, not realizing the enormous amount of work weeding such a garden would entail. Despite my naïveté, I managed to harvest a bumper crop. I can't begin to count the many daikon dishes I created and served to my hosts. So as not to waste the surplus, we pickled the remainder, and by the end of the year we gave them as gladly received Christmas gifts.*

Although this salad is very easy to make, the combination of lime juice, sugar, and the mustardy flavor of daikon makes it remarkably exotic.

One 1 1/2-pound daikon, peeled and cut into
   1/8-inch-thick slices
2 tablespoons granulated sugar
1/4 cup fresh lime juice
1 green onion, thinly sliced

In a bowl, combine all the ingredients and toss to mix well.

Serves 4.

Tobu Peipinpout Thoke
Bean Curd Cake and Bean Sprout Salad

This salad is sold in food stalls in Rangoon as a snack. I recommend frying your own bean curd rather than buying the prefried variety. Be sure to purchase firm rather than soft bean curd.

1 package (19 ounces) firm bean curd cake
3 cups vegetable oil
1 large yellow onion
1/4 teaspoon ground turmeric
3 tablespoons chana dal powder
2 cups mung bean sprouts
2 tablespoons freshly squeezed lime juice
1 teaspoon salt
1/2 cup thinly chopped green onion
1/4 teaspoon crushed dried red chile pepper

Pat the bean curd cake dry with absorbent paper towels. Heat 2 cups of the oil in a frying pan over medium-high heat. Add the bean curd cake and fry until golden brown on the first side, about 7 minutes. Turn and fry on the second side until golden brown, about 7 minutes. Remove the bean curd cake from the pan with a slotted utensil. Cut into 1/2-inch-thick slices and set aside.

Slice the yellow onion in half vertically and then slice the halves thinly to form crescent-shaped fans. Heat the remaining 1 cup oil in a frying pan over medium heat. Add the onion and turmeric and sauté until golden brown, about 6 minutes. Drain the onion, reserving 2 tablespoons of the oil, and set the onion and oil aside.

Heat a small dry frying pan over medium heat. Add the chana dal powder and stir constantly until light brown, about 3 minutes.

In a large bowl, combine the bean curd, onion and oil, toasted dal powder, and all the remaining ingredients. Mix well.

Serves 4.

Syaukthee Thoke
Grapefruit Salad

Burmese eat this salad because of its invigorating qualities. Despite the effort involved in removing the fruit from its casing, this dish is well worth the labor.

2 large grapefruit
1 large yellow onion
1 cup vegetable oil
1/4 teaspoon ground turmeric
3 tablespoons chana dal powder
1/4 cup shrimp powder
1/4 teaspoon salt
1/2 cup thinly sliced green onion

Peel the grapefruit and separate them into sections. With your fingers, gently remove the membrane that encases each section. Put the sections in a colander to drain while you prepare the remaining ingredients.

Cut the yellow onion in half vertically and then slice thinly to form crescent-shaped fans. Heat the oil in a skillet over medium heat. Add the onion and sauté until golden brown, about 6 minutes. Drain the onion, reserving 2 tablespoons of the oil, and set the onion and oil aside.

Heat a small, dry frying pan over medium heat. Add the chana dal powder and stir constantly until light brown, about 3 minutes.

In a large bowl, combine the grapefruit, onion and oil, toasted dal powder, and all the remaining ingredients. Mix well.

Serves 4.

Thinnbawthee Thoke
Green Papaya Salad

During my early years in San Francisco, I tried in vain to find green papayas. Most grocers thought I was crazy asking for unripened fruit. Thanks to the city's burgeoning Southeast Asian community, I am now able to find just about all the fruits and vegetables I had back home. These days, not only do I find green papayas, but for a few pennies more, I can have the grocer shred them for me. And now no one thinks I am crazy.

1 yellow onion
1/2 cup vegetable oil
1/4 teaspoon ground turmeric
4 cups green papaya, peeled and shredded (about 1 pound)
1/4 cup shrimp powder
2 tablespoons fresh lime juice

Cut the onion in half vertically and then slice thinly to form crescent-shaped fans. Heat the oil in a frying pan over medium heat. Add the onion and turmeric and sauté until golden brown, about 6 minutes. Drain the onion, reserving 2 tablespoons of the oil.

In a large bowl, combine the onion and oil and all the remaining ingredients. Mix well.

Serves 4.

Laphet

Pickled Tea Leaf Salad

Laphet *is a type of pickled tea leaf. It is made by lightly steaming young tea leaves and then pressing them tightly into clay vessels or large bamboo stems and storing the containers in the ground, preferably close to a river bed to ensure a steady temperature.* Laphet *comes from Burma's great central city of Mandalay. Because of the way in which this recipe is prepared, we call it a salad, but it is actually a dessert and is always eaten after a meal. Burmese restaurants in San Francisco offer it as a first course because their non-Burmese patrons would find it a very uncommon dessert, but such a practice would be taboo in Burma.*

There are two levels of conversation at a Burmese meal: social welfare before dinner, and religious and political topics after dinner. Since laphet *is somewhat of a stimulant, it goes well with the latter. We either make the salad at home or go to eat it in shops that have atmospheres similar to those of Western cafes. Although these pickled tea leaves cannot be found in any American stores, this dish is available at Burmese restaurants. Or you should make friends with some Burmese. Connections are the key.*

2 tablespoons sesame seed
1/4 cup *laphet*
3 tablespoons vegetable oil
1/4 teaspoon salt
1/2 cup dried shrimp
2 cloves garlic, thinly sliced
1/2 cup roasted and skinned peanuts
1 cup fried broad beans or lima beans

Heat a small, dry frying pan over medium heat. Add the sesame seed and stir constantly until the seeds are light brown and begin to pop, about 3 minutes.

In a bowl, combine the sesame seed with all the remaining ingredients. Mix well.

Serves 4.

Ghin Thoke

Pickled Ginger Salad

Like the tea leaf salad, this ginger salad is a much-liked dessert. It, too, is found in small shops where you can sit down and enjoy it with tea or have it packed for take-out. Most people eat this salad during the day; the tea leaf salad is preferred at night.

The best pickled ginger to use for this dish is labeled "kizami shoga" and is available in jars in Japanese and other Asian markets. You must squeeze out all of the liquid before measuring the ginger. The fried yellow split peas are labeled "chana fried" and can be found in markets carrying Indian goods.

1 tablespoon sesame seed
1/4 cup well-drained sliced pickled ginger (*kizami shoga*)
1/2 cup fried yellow split peas
1/2 cup coarsely crushed, roasted and skinned peanuts
1/4 teaspoon salt
2 tablespoons shrimp powder
1 clove garlic, thinly sliced
1 tablespoon corn oil

Heat a small, dry frying pan over medium heat. Add the sesame seed and stir constantly until the seeds are light brown and begin to pop, about 3 minutes.

In a bowl, combine the sesame seed and all the remaining ingredients. Mix well.

Serves 4.

Kaukswe Thoke
Noodle Salad

Made in quantity, this can be a great party dish. It's also good for picnics, as it can be easily packed for carrying. Serve with fried chicken wings and cucumber slices.

2 pounds fresh Chinese chow mein noodles (^{1}/8 inch thick)
1 tablespoon plus 1 cup vegetable oil
1 large yellow onion
^{1}/4 teaspoon ground turmeric
^{1}/2 cup chana dal powder
^{1}/2 cup finely chopped green onion
5 tablespoons freshly squeezed lime juice
1 tablespoon salt, or to taste
3 tablespoons fish sauce

Fill a large saucepan with water and bring to a boil. Add the 1 tablespoon oil and the noodles and cook until tender, 4 to 5 minutes. Drain, rinse under cold running water, and drain again. Transfer to a large serving bowl.

Meanwhile, cut the onion in half vertically and then slice the halves thinly to form crescent-shaped fans. Heat the oil in a frying pan over medium heat. Add the onion and turmeric and sauté until golden brown, about 6 minutes. Drain the onion, reserving ^{1}/2 cup of the oil, and set the onion and oil aside.

Heat a small, dry skillet over medium heat. Add the chana dal powder and stir constantly until light brown, about 4 minutes.

Add the onion and oil, toasted dal powder, green onion, and lime juice to the noodles. Mix well.

Serves 6.

Kyarzan Thoke
Bean Thread Noodle Salad

The bean thread, or silver, noodle is widely used in Burma. and this dish is as popular as the Burmese salad made with Chinese Chow mein on page 158. With a bowl of hot Bottleneck Gourd Soup (page 40), you have a complete meal.

2 medium-sized potatoes, peeled and cut into eighths
10 $^1/_2$ ounces bean thread noodles
1 large yellow onion
1 cup vegetable oil
$^1/_4$ teaspoon ground turmeric
6 tablespoons chana dal powder
$^1/_2$ cup finely sliced green onion
$^1/_4$ cup fresh lemon juice
1 teaspoon ground lemongrass
3 tablespoons fish sauce
$^1/_2$ teaspoon salt

Place the potatoes in a saucepan, add water to cover, bring to a boil, and boil until tender but still firm, 15 to 20 minutes. Drain and set aside to cool.

Meanwhile, fill a saucepan with water, bring to a boil, add the noodles, and boil until tender and glassy in appearance, about 15 minutes; drain and set aside to cool.

While the potatoes and noodles are cooking, cut the yellow onion in half vertically and then thinly slice to form crescent-shaped fans. Heat the oil in a frying pan over medium heat. Add the onion and turmeric and sauté until golden brown, about 6 minutes. Drain the onion, reserving $^1/_4$ cup of the oil, and set the onion and oil aside.

Heat a small, dry frying pan over medium heat. Add the chana dal powder and stir constantly until light brown, about 4 minutes.

In a large bowl, combine the potatoes, noodles, onion and oil, toasted dal powder, and all the remaining ingredients. Mix well.

Serves 4.

This salad takes its inspiration from one popular in the Tenasserim area, the southern strip of Burma that borders Thailand. Any shellfish you choose works equally well.

1 1/2 pounds shrimp, peeled and deveined
1 yellow onion
4 cloves garlic, thinly sliced
1 1/2 tablespoons vegetable oil
3 tablespoons fresh lime juice
1 1/2 teaspoons salt
1/4 cup thinly sliced green onion

Fill a saucepan with water and bring to a boil. Add the shrimp and cook until they curl slightly and turn pink, about 1 minute. Remove from the heat, drain, and let cool. Cut each shrimp in half lengthwise along the back. Place in a large bowl.

Cut the yellow onion in half vertically and then slice thinly to form crescent-shaped fans. Add the onion to the shrimp, along with all the remaining ingredients. Mix well.

Serves 4.

A good accompaniment to any full-course meal. American friends sometimes add shredded cabbage or lettuce (about half a cup) and serve this dish alone as a light entrée.

1 ¹/2 pounds shrimp, peeled and deveined
1 large yellow onion
1 cup vegetable oil
¹/4 teaspoon ground turmeric
2 tablespoons chana dal powder
3 tablespoons fresh lime juice
¹/2 teaspoon salt
¹/4 cup thinly sliced green onion
1 tablespoon finely chopped fresh cilantro

Fill a saucepan with water and bring to a boil. Add the shrimp and cook just until they curl slightly and turn pink, about 1 minute. Remove from the heat, drain, and let cool. Cut each shrimp in half lengthwise along the back. Set aside.

Cut the yellow onion in half vertically and then slice the halves thinly to form crescent-shaped fans. Heat the oil in a frying pan over medium heat. Add the onion and turmeric and sauté until golden brown, about 6 minutes. Drain the onion, reserving 2 tablespoons of the oil, and set the onion and oil aside.

Heat a small, dry frying pan over medium heat. Add the chana dal powder and stir constantly until light brown, about 3 minutes.

In a large bowl, combine the shrimp, onion and oil, toasted dal powder, lime juice, salt, green onion, and cilantro. Mix well.

Serves 4.

Pyegyee Ngar Thoke
Squid Salad

I developed this dish in the United States when I discovered the small, tender, delicious squid available here. In Burma I never ate fresh squid. What was used instead was dried squid imported from China, which the Burmese call Pyegyeengar. (Pyegyee means "big country," for China, and ngar means "fish.") You may wonder why Burma imported squid from China when the whole Bay of Bengal was at its doorstep. Although people in the coastal fishing villages regularly cooked squid straight from the sea, the inland Burmese were skeptical of fish brought in from the coast. Since Burma is a land of many rivers, freshwater fish were preferred, and perhaps the Burmese also felt that seafood smelled "fishier." In the early fifties, the Martaban Fishing Company introduced seafood to the inland Burmese. Even then it took nearly two decades to convince us.

1 1/2 pounds squid
3 1/2 teaspoons salt, or to taste
1 yellow onion
1 cup vegetable oil
1/4 teaspoon ground turmeric
1/2 cup chana dal powder
3 tablespoons sesame seed
2 tablespoons fresh lime juice
2 tablespoons finely minced fresh cilantro
1/4 cup thinly sliced green onion
1/4 teaspoon crushed dried red chile pepper

Cut off the tentacles from each squid just above the eyes. Squeeze the bulbous part of the tentacles to push out the hard beak; discard the beak and set the tentacles aside in a bowl. Slit the body of each squid from eyes to tail. Remove the head, entrails, ink sac, and cuttlebone and discard. Peel off the mottled skin. Slice the body crosswise into 1/2-inch-wide strips. Place the squid strips in the bowl with the tentacles and 2 teaspoons of the salt. Using your hands, mix until a foamy substance appears, then drain in a colander and rinse thoroughly with cold running water.

Fill a saucepan with water and bring to a boil. Add the squid and boil for 1 minute. Drain and set aside.

Cut the onion in half vertically and then slice the halves thinly to form crescent-shaped fans. Heat the oil in a frying pan over medium heat. Add the onion and turmeric and sauté until golden brown, about 6 minutes. Drain the onion, reserving 3 tablespoons of the oil, and set the onion and oil aside.

Heat a small, dry frying pan over medium heat. Add the chana dal powder and stir constantly until light brown, about 4 minutes. Remove the powder from the skillet and set aside. In the same skillet over medium heat, toast the sesame seed, stirring constantly, until the seeds are light brown and begin to pop, 3 to 4 minutes.

In a large bowl, combine the squid, onion and oil, toasted dal powder, sesame seed, lime juice, cilantro, green onion, chile pepper, and the remaining 1 1/2 teaspoons salt. Mix well.

Serves 4.

Ngaphare Thoke
Ladyfish Salad

Here is another recipe that calls for the same fish paste found in Chinese markets that I use to make the Ladyfish Ball Curry on page 125.

Vegetable oil for rubbing on hands, plus
   2 cups vegetable oil for cooking
1 pound ladyfish paste
1 large yellow onion
1/4 teaspoon ground turmeric
1/4 cup chana dal powder
1/2 cup diced green onion
1 tablespoon finely minced fresh cilantro
1/4 cup fresh lemon juice
1 tablespoon fish sauce
1 teaspoon minced medium-hot fresh green chile pepper

Rub a generous amount of oil on both hands to reduce the stickiness of working with the fish paste. Form the fish paste into small patties about 2 inches in diameter and 1/4 inch thick.

Heat 1 cup of the oil in a frying pan over medium heat. Add the patties and fry on both sides until golden brown and cooked through, about 2 minutes on each side. Remove the patties with a slotted utensil to absorbent paper towels to drain; let cool and then slice thinly crosswise. Set aside.

Cut the onion in half vertically and then slice the halves thinly to form crescent-shaped fans. Heat the remaining 1 cup oil in a frying pan over medium heat. Add the onion and turmeric and sauté until golden brown, about 6 minutes. Drain the onion, reserving 2 tablespoons of the oil, and set the onion and oil aside.

Heat a small, dry frying pan over medium heat. Add the chana dal powder and stir constantly until light brown, about 4 minutes.

In a large bowl, combine fish slices, onion and oil, toasted dal powder, and all the remaining ingredients. Mix well.

Serves 4.

Kyethar Thoke
Chicken Salad

An authentic chicken salad sold in Burma's food bazaars consists of chopped boiled intestines, livers, gizzards, heads, wing tips, feet, and skin. Thank God the feathers are used for pillows. I personally prefer to use leftover roast chicken. This salad is perfect served with steamed rice for a light lunch.

1 yellow onion
1 cup vegetable oil
$1/4$ teaspoon ground turmeric
3 tablespoons chana dal powder
1 cucumber
2 cups shredded, cooked chicken meat
2 tablespoons fresh lime juice
1 tablespoon fish sauce
$1/4$ teaspoon salt
$1/2$ cup thinly sliced green onion

Cut the yellow onion in half vertically and then slice the halves thinly to form crescent-shaped fans. Heat the oil in a frying pan over medium heat. Add the onion and turmeric and sauté until golden brown, about 6 minutes. Drain the onion, reserving 3 tablespoons of the oil, and set the onion and oil aside.

Heat a small, dry frying pan over medium heat. Add the chana dal powder and stir constantly until light brown, about 3 minutes; set aside.

Peel the cucumber and cut in half lengthwise. Scrape out and discard the seeds and cut the cucumber into thin slices.

In a large bowl, combine the onion and oil, toasted dal powder, cucumber, and all the remaining ingredients. Mix well.

Serves 4.

Whethar Thoke

Pork Salad with Cucumber

The cucumber and lemon juice add a cool, light contrast to the pork. Fried Rice (page 197) is an especially good accompaniment.

1 1/2 pounds lean pork butt, in one piece
1 cucumber
1 yellow onion
2 tablespoons fresh lime juice
2 tablespoons finely minced fresh cilantro
1/2 teaspoon salt
2 cloves garlic, finely minced

Place the pork in a saucepan and add water to cover. Bring to a boil, reduce the heat, and simmer until the pork is cooked, 45 minutes to 1 hour. Remove the pork from the pan and let cool to room temperature. Cut the pork into narrow strips measuring 2 inches long and 1/8 inch thick; set aside.

Peel the cucumber and cut it in half lengthwise. Scoop out and discard the seeds. Cut the cucumber into 1/8-inch-thick slices. Cut the onion in half vertically and then slice thinly to form crescent-shaped fans.

In a large bowl, combine the pork, cucumber, onion, and all the remaining ingredients. Toss to mix well.

Serves 4.

Whetnaywet Thoke
Pig's Ear Salad

Pigs are the only animals whose ears the Burmese eat. The soft crunch of the cartilage gives an unusual sensation—different from any other food. The mild flavor of the ears make them a good foil for a variety of different sauces.

3 1/2 to 4 quarts water
5 pig's ears
1/4 cup vegetable oil
4 cloves garlic, finely minced
1 yellow onion
2 tablespoons fish sauce
3 tablespoons fresh lime juice

In a large saucepan, combine the water and pig's ears, bring to a boil, reduce the heat, cover, and simmer until the ears are tender but still have crunch, 1 1/2 hours. Drain the ears and let cool. Cut the ears into slices 2 inches long and 3/8 inch wide and set aside in a large bowl.

Heat the oil in a frying pan over medium heat. Add the garlic and sauté until golden brown, about 1 minute. Drain the garlic, reserving 1 teaspoon of the oil. Add the garlic and oil to the bowl holding the ears.

Cut the onion in half vertically and then slice thinly to form crescent-shaped fans. Add the onion, fish sauce, and lime juice to the ears. Mix well.

Serves 4.

Whetnaywet Thoke II
Pig's Ear Salad with Sriracha Chile Sauce

In this recipe the pig's ears are mixed with crunchy cucumber for added texture. The Sriracha chili sauce, named for a Thai coastal town, adds a hot, slightly sweet tang to the dish. For a less spicy salad, prepare Garlic and Vinegar Sauce (page 21) and toss the sliced pig's ears with the sauce, omitting the cucumbers and onion.

3 1/2 to 4 quarts water
5 pig's ears
2 cucumbers
1/2 yellow onion
5 tablespoons Sriracha chile sauce

In a large saucepan, combine the water and pig's ears, bring to a boil, reduce the heat, cover, and simmer until the ears are tender but still have crunch, 1 1/2 hours. Drain the ears and let cool. Cut the ears into slices 2 inches long and 3/8 inch wide and set aside in a large bowl.

Peel the cucumbers and cut them in half lengthwise. Scrape and discard the seeds. Slice the cucumbers thinly. Thinly slice the onion half to form crescent-shaped fans.

Add the cucumbers, onion, and chile sauce to the bowl. Mix well.

Serves 4.

Most Burmese who live on the outskirts of towns or in rural areas grow their own vegetables. Various kinds of gourds are particularly popular and are grown on pergolas near the house. Water spinach is also commonly cultivated, usually in a nearby small pond.

The Karen tribesmen who live along the Salween River in southwestern Burma are especially renowned for their knowledge of vegetables and herbs. One summer, I visited a Karen friend at his village. Every morning he would take me through the jungle for the salad hunt. It was like taking a field trip with a botany teacher. In a short time, I was able to absorb seemingly endless information about rare edible plants from his encyclopedic mind. While we talked, his brothers were out in the jungle hunting for the main course. Compared to the city life I led in Rangoon, their's seemed idyllic. Yet in Burma, many people still practice this way of life as the only means to survive.

Today, walking along the aisles in the produce section of a supermarket, I often wonder whether the Burmese really belong to the twentieth century.

Hintheesone Kala Hin
Mixed Vegetable Curry

I always prepare this dish when my vegetarian friends come for dinner. In Rangoon we jokingly called it Chettyars' curry because it is meatless and was what poor Burmese farmers who worked for the Chettyars could afford. The Chettyars are members of a caste of south Indian merchants and money lenders who owned vast tracts of Burma's farmland when the country was under British rule.

1/2 cup vegetable oil
1 yellow onion, finely diced
1/2 teaspoon ground turmeric
1 1/2 teaspoons salt
2 tablespoons ground cumin
1 tablespoon ground coriander
1 tablespoon paprika
2 bay leaves
1 1/2 cups yellow split peas, cooked in boiling water to cover
   until tender (about 45 minutes) and drained
1/2 cup tamarind juice
2 cups sliced, peeled daikon (1/4-inch-thick slices)
One 1 pound eggplant, cut into 2-inch squares
   about 1 inch thick
3 medium-sized red potatoes peeled and cut into quarters
4 cups peeled pumpkin squares (2-inch squares about
   1-inch thick)
3 medium-sized carrots, peeled and cut into 2-inch lengths
1 tablespoon finely minced fresh cilantro
4 cups water

Heat the oil in a large saucepan over medium heat. Add the onion and sauté until it begins to soften, 3 minutes. Add the turmeric, salt, cumin, coriander, paprika, bay leaves, and cooked split peas. Cover and simmer for 5 minutes, stirring frequently.

Add the tamarind juice, daikon, eggplant, potatoes, pumpkin, carrots, cilantro, and water. Cover and simmer until the vegetables are tender, about 30 minutes.
Serves 6.

Shwephayonethee Hin
Pumpkin Curry

Many years ago I spent Halloween with a family in Petaluma, California. The next day, in an act of gratitude, I cooked this dish for their dinner. I wasn't prepared when the kids threw a fit because I'd destroyed their jack-o'-lantern.

One 3-pound pumpkin
$1/2$ cup vegetable oil
1 yellow onion, finely chopped
1 tablespoon finely minced garlic
1 teaspoon ground turmeric
1 $1/2$ teaspoons salt
1 tablespoon paprika
3 cups water
1 $1/2$ tablespoons finely chopped fresh parsley

Cut the pumpkin in half and scrape out and discard the seeds and fibers. Peel the skin with a sharp knife. Cut the pulp into 2-inch squares about 1 inch thick; set aside.

Heat the oil in a large frying pan over medium-low heat. Add the onion, garlic, and turmeric and sauté until they just begin to soften, about 3 minutes.

Add the pumpkin, salt, paprika, and water. Cover and simmer over medium heat until water is reduced to $1/2$ cup and the pumpkin is tender, about 30 minutes. Transfer to a serving dish and garnish with parsley.

Serves 4.

Monastery cooks are not necessarily good cooks. More often than not, they are volunteers and are faced with having to concoct dishes from ingredients donated to the monastery. But when they concocted this dish, they created something excellent, which is rarely the case. I've regularly visited monasteries during my painting trips, and, through the kindness of the head monks, I was frequently invited to dine with them. This curry was commonly among the many dishes served.

In Burma lima beans are dried and have to be soaked in water overnight before cooking. Thanks to the ingenuity of the West, one can purchase perfectly cooked and perfectly shaped lima beans in a can. I am certain that the chefs from those faraway monasteries would gladly accept a can or two.

> 5 tablespoons vegetable oil
> 1 yellow onion, finely chopped
> $1/2$ teaspoon ground turmeric
> 2 cans (17 ounces each) lima beans or
>   butter beans, drained
> 1 teaspoon salt
> 1 cup water
> 1 cup finely sliced green onion

Heat the oil in a saucepan over medium-low heat. Add the yellow onion and turmeric and sauté until the onion is translucent, about 5 minutes.

Add the beans and salt and stir gently for 3 minutes. Add the water, cover, and simmer until liquid is reduced to $1/2$ cup, about 15 minutes. Transfer to a serving dish and garnish with the green onion.

Serves 4.

Kyethingarthee Hin

Bitter Melon or Bitter Gourd Curry

The Welsh actor Richard Burton once said, "I've never met anybody interesting who didn't drink." I feel the same way about people who won't try unusual foods such as bitter melon. People who are adventurous in their eating are never boring.

3 1/2 pounds bitter melons
1/4 cup vegetable oil
1 yellow onion, finely chopped
1/4 teaspoon ground turmeric
2 medium-sized beefsteak tomatoes,
    cut into eighths
3 tablespoons shrimp powder
1 teaspoon salt
1 1/2 teaspoons paprika
1/4 teaspoon granulated sugar
2 cups water

Cut the bitter melons in half lengthwise and scrape out and discard the seeds and the membrane surrounding them. Cut the melon into 1/4-inch-thick slices.

Heat the oil in a saucepan over medium heat. Add the onion and turmeric and sauté until the onion begins to soften, 3 minutes. Add the tomatoes and shrimp powder and sauté until the tomatoes soften, about 10 minutes. Add the bitter melons, salt, paprika, sugar, and water. Cover and simmer, stirring frequently, until the liquid is reduced to 1/2 cup, about 20 minutes.

Serves 4.

Buthee Taw Chet
Bottleneck Gourd Curry

This recipe is a step up from the way very poor families prepare the same curry in Burma. They call their version gourd curry with water. I ate it many times during painting trips to the villages, and every time I did, I saw the harsh realities of life more clearly.

One 2-pound bottleneck gourd
4 teaspoons vegetable oil
1 yellow onion, finely chopped
1/4 teaspoon ground turmeric
1 tablespoon fish sauce
3/4 teaspoon salt
1 1/2 teaspoons paprika
2 cups water

Peel the gourd. Cut in half lengthwise and scrape out and discard the seeds and pith. Cut the gourd into 2-inch squares about 1 inch thick.

Heat the oil in a frying pan over medium heat. Add the onion and turmeric and sauté until the onion begins to soften, 3 minutes. Add the gourd pieces, fish sauce, salt, and paprika. Cook, stirring for 3 minutes. Add the water, cover, and simmer until the liquid is reduced to 1/2 cup, about 30 minutes.

Serves 4.

Khayanthee Hin
Eggplant Curry

I was delighted to learn that there are so many delicious recipes from all over the world devoted to the eggplant. I was shocked, however, to discover how few people in America eat this wonderful vegetable-like fruit. I think this situation has more to do with the difficulty of preparing some eggplant dishes than it does with the taste of the eggplant itself. This dish belongs at the center of authentic Burmese cuisine and once made will change even the most stubborn protester into an avid fan of this neglected food.

    1 teaspoon salt
    1 teaspoon ground turmeric
    One 1 1/2-pound globe eggplant, peeled and
       cut into eighths lengthwise
    1/4 cup vegetable oil
    1 yellow onion, finely chopped
    1 tablespoon finely minced garlic
    1/2 cup shrimp powder
    1 tablespoon paprika
    1 tablespoon fish sauce
    3 cups water

Rub the salt and turmeric on the eggplant pieces, evenly coating them.

Heat the oil in a skillet over medium-low heat. Add the onion, garlic, shrimp powder, and paprika and sauté until the onion begins to soften, about 3 minutes. Add the eggplant and stir to mix in evenly. Cook for 3 minutes, stirring frequently. Add the water, cover, and simmer until the liquid is reduced to 1/2 cup, about 30 minutes.

Serves 4.

Ahloo Masala
Spiced Potatoes with Fried Onions

My Irish friend John Norton throws an annual St. Patrick's Day party, a real corned beef and cabbage affair. One year he asked me to do the potatoes. This dish managed to make many an Irish eyebrow rise.

> 7 medium-sized red potatoes,
> peeled and cut into eighths
> 1 large yellow onion
> 1 cup vegetable oil
> 1/4 teaspoon ground turmeric
> 5 tablespoons ground cumin
> 2 teaspoons salt
> 1 tablespoon ground coriander
> 2 tablespoons paprika
> 1/2 cup thinly sliced green onion
> 1/2 teaspoon ground black pepper

Place the potatoes in a saucepan and add water to cover. Bring to a boil and boil until tender but still firm, 15 to 20 minutes. Drain and set aside to cool to room temperature.

Cut the yellow onion in half vertically and then slice the halves thinly to form crescent-shaped fans. Heat the oil in a frying pan over medium heat. Add the onion and turmeric and sauté until golden brown, about 6 minutes. Remove from the heat and set aside to cool to room temperature.

In a large bowl, combine the potatoes, onion and oil, and all the remaining ingredients. Mix well.

Serves 4.

Myit Kyaw
Fried Bamboo Shoots

Although there are hundreds of species of bamboo in Burma, the real art comes in knowing when a shoot is ready to pick for eating. You can't pick a bamboo shoot simply because you see it growing out of the ground. It could be too young or too old for the kitchen. In my travels around Burma, I once met a girl who knew the bamboo forests by heart. Pointing a finger at a shoot she would say to me, "This one here has two days more to go, that one there has five days, and this one we'll come and get tomorrow morning." Although at the time I was more interested in her than in learning how to pick bamboo shoots, her knowledge and love of bamboo-shoot picking held me in good stead later in life, especially in hikes through the jungle.

1/4 cup vegetable oil
1/2 cup shrimp powder
1/4 teaspoon ground turmeric
1 1/2 pounds fresh bamboo shoots,
   shredded and well drained
1 tablespoon paprika
1/8 teaspoon salt
1/2 cup water

Heat the oil in a frying pan over medium heat. Add the shrimp powder and turmeric and sauté for 15 seconds. Add the bamboo shoots, paprika, and salt and stir-fry for 5 minutes. Add the water, cover, and simmer, stirring frequently, until the liquid evaporates, about 5 minutes. Uncover and cook for 5 minutes, stirring frequently.

Serves 4.

Gawrakhar Thee Kyaw
Stir-Fried Chayote Squash

The Burmese named the chayote squash after the Gurkhas, the dominant race of Nepal. A branch of these people live in Burma, and although they are well known as fierce warriors, they are also kind and loving by nature. You'll notice the exterior of a chayote squash is firm and rigid. But its flesh is sweet and friendly to the taste, just as the Gurkhas are.

4 medium-sized chayote squash
2 tablespoons vegetable oil
1 1/2 tablespoons water
1/4 teaspoon salt
1/4 teaspoon ground black pepper

Peel the squash. Cut in half lengthwise and remove the large flat seed. Cut the halves lengthwise into 3/8-inch-thick slices, then cut the slices into 3/8-inch-thick strips.

Heat the oil in a frying pan over medium-high heat. Add the squash and sauté for 1 minute. Add the water and simmer, uncovered, until the water evaporates, about 1 minute. Add the salt and pepper and cook, stirring frequently, for 1 minute.

Serves 4.

Kazunywet Kyaw
Stir-Fried Water Spinach

The first letter of the Burmese alphabet is pronounced ka. *And this plant is called* kazunpin. *American children are taught* A *is for apple,* B *is for ball,* C *is for cat and* D *is for doll. Burmese teach their alphabet to their children by starting with* ka *and singing, "Ka, kazunpin ye mhar shin." It means "Ka for kazunpin, the plant is alive and happy in the water."*

1 1/2 pounds water spinach
4 cloves garlic - crushed flat
  using the side of a cleaver
3 tablespoons vegetable oil
1 tablespoon Asian sesame oil
1/2 teaspoon salt
1 tablespoon light soy sauce
1/4 teaspoon ground black pepper

Pick off the leaves of the spinach and break the tender stem portions into 3-inch-long pieces. Heat the oils in a large frying pan over high heat. Add the garlic and stir-fry for 15 seconds. Quickly add the spinach leaves and stems, salt, soy sauce, and pepper and stir-fry over very high heat until the spinach is just tender, about 30 seconds.

Serves 4.

Chinbaung Kyaw
Rhubarb and Spinach Paste

The chinbaung *plant grows almost everywhere in Burma, and its leaves are essential for making this dish. Easy if you are in Burma, but if you are in a place where there's absolutely no chinbaung plant, one can only long for it. That was what I did in San Francisco, until my mother discovered rhubarb, which tastes almost identical to* chinbaung *leaves. We have fooled our Burmese friends many times by passing off rhubarb as* chinbaung. *I have also served this dish to many American friends who rarely eat rhubarb. They were uniformly pleased and surprised to learn afterward that this tasty concoction was made from the often-scorned vegetable.*

> 5 tablespoons vegetable oil
> 1 yellow onion, finely chopped
> 1/4 teaspoon ground turmeric
> 2 1/2 pounds rhubarb stalks,
>   peeled of all fibrous threads
>   and cut into 2-inch lengths
> 2 bunches spinach, stems trimmed
> 1/4 cup shrimp powder
> 1 tablespoon paprika
> 1 tablespoon fish sauce
> 1/4 teaspoon salt
> 1 cup water

Heat the oil in a 2-inch-deep frying pan over medium heat. Add the onion and turmeric and sauté until the onion begins to soften, 3 minutes.

Add the rhubarb and spinach and sauté until the rhubarb softens and the spinach wilts, about 10 minutes. Mash the rhubarb with a slotted spoon. Add all the remaining ingredients, cover, and simmer over low heat, stirring frequently, until the liquid is reduced to 1/4 cup, about 15 minutes.

Serves 4.

Kyayanchinthee Cyet
Tomato Sauce

A menu consisting of this sauce, fried meat or fish, mango slices, gourd soup, and steamed rice is the most classic provincial dinner a Burmese could wish for. The sauce acts as a flavorful gravy to wet the rice. It also goes very well with spaghetti.

5 tablespoons vegetable oil
1 yellow onion, finely chopped
$1/4$ teaspoon ground turmeric
1 tablespoon minced garlic
6 medium-sized beefsteak tomatoes,
    cut into eighths
1 tablespoon fish sauce
1 tablespoon paprika
8 sprigs fresh cilantro
2 cups water

Heat the oil in a saucepan over medium heat. Add the onion, turmeric, and garlic and sauté until the onion begins to soften, about 3 minutes. Add the tomatoes, fish sauce, and paprika and simmer, stirring frequently, until the tomatoes are soft, about 10 minutes. Add the cilantro and water, cover, and simmer covered until the liquid is reduced to $1/2$ cup, about 20 minutes.

Serves 4.

The mango pickle of India is also popular in Burma. My mother used to make big batches of it and pack it in jars, to give as gifts to friends. In America we couldn't maintain the tradition because of the rarity and high expense of the particular green mango that must be used. Instead of mango pickle, my mother created this truly wonderful pickle using cauliflower. It will keep for two weeks in a jar in the refrigerator.

1 medium-sized cauliflower (about 2 pounds)
1 teaspoon ground turmeric
1 tablespoon plus 1/2 teaspoon granulated sugar
1 tablespoon plus about 1 1/2 teaspoons salt
1/2 cup distilled white vinegar
1 cup vegetable oil
1 tablespoon black mustard seed
1/2 cup ground cumin
1/4 cup ground coriander
1 tablespoon ground fenugreek
1 teaspoon ground cardamom
1 1/2 tablespoons paprika
15 cloves garlic, cut lengthwise into quarters
1 tablespoon julienned fresh ginger

Cut the florets from the cauliflower, leaving a 1-inch stem on each floret. Make sure that all of the florets are bite-sized.

Fill a large saucepan with water and bring to a boil. Add the turmeric, the 1 tablespoon sugar, the 1 tablespoon salt, and vinegar. Boil for 30 seconds. Add the florets and blanch for 1 minute. Drain the florets and let cool completely.

Heat the oil in large saucepan over medium heat. Add the mustard seed, cumin, coriander, fenugreek, cardamom, and paprika. Stir constantly for 30 seconds, then quickly add the cauliflower, the 1 1/2 teaspoons salt, the 1/2 teaspoon sugar, garlic, and ginger. Stir thoroughly so that all of the ingredients are evenly mixed. Adjust the seasoning with salt, if necessary.

Serves 4.

Mandalay, the second largest city in Burma, is the Mecca of Burmese culture. I traveled by train to Mandalay on many occasions, as it was a perfect environment for a young artist to work. There I would spend most of my time painting and then return to Rangoon for an exhibition.

During those journeys, all one saw from the train window were endless paddy fields and proud farmers, with their villages and tiny white stupas resting on far-off hills. This vision has taught me about the enlightenment of the proud and jubilant soul.

Rice is the life blood of Burma and the farmers who are devoted to its cultivation are considered the country's most honorable citizens. With its flat lands and tropical weather and rain, Burma is ideally suited for growing rice. The Irrawaddy delta and the lower valleys of the Sittang and Salween rivers are devoted to rice farming.

There are over one hundred varieties of rice grown in Burma; the most popular are *nga kywe, san hmwe, emahtut, yargyaw, ziyar, medon, zagwe, nga sein,* and *lonedei.* Their price and taste vary. *Nga kywe* is the most expensive and the easiest to digest. It is the favorite for the table of the wealthy. *Nga sein,* which has a harder texture when cooked and is less expensive, is eaten by the farmers. *Londei* is the hardest and cheapest and mainly used in feeding the inmates of prisons and livestock. Many of the other varieties, such as the sweet, pink, and black rices, are used in making snacks and confections.

Before World War II, Burma was the world's largest exporter of rice. In the early sixties, after the military takeover, prewar export figures tumbled to less than 2 million tons; by 1969, the tonnage had dropped to 350,000. I remember that year vividly; we had to wait in line holding a rice ration card.

Today, the government claims that rice production is setting new records, but in reality there isn't enough rice to go around, not even for the farmers who grow it. It is a sad state of affairs when the Burmese people are forced to buy rice from black marketeers, much like a gardener who can't pick the flowers in his own garden.

To enjoy Burmese food at its most authentic, all the recipes in this book should be eaten with long-grain white rice. Brown rice isn't suited to these dishes.

There are two ways to cook rice. In the first method, which is common in Burma, the rice is boiled with a generous amount of water and then the starchy water is drained off. The cooked rice has little starch and the Burmese use the milky water for starching clothes or for animal feed. In the second method, which is popular in the United States, the rice is cooked in far less water and works on the same principle as the electric rice cooker.

2 cups long-grain white rice, well rinsed and drained

Method 1: Combine the rice and 3 quarts of water in a large saucepan. Bring to a boil over medium heat and cook, uncovered, for 15 minutes. Place a lid on the pan to trap the rice, tip the pan, and carefully drain the water off completely. Cover the pan, place over very low heat, and cook for 15 minutes.

Method 2: Place the rice in a medium-sized pan and shake the pan to level the surface of the rice. Add water slowly until it reaches 1 inch above the level of the rice. Bring to a boil over medium heat and cook, uncovered, for 1 minute. Reduce the heat to very low, cover, and cook for 20 minutes.

Serves 4.

Peihtamin
Yellow Split Pea Rice

Indians are very innovative in their preparation of elaborate rice dishes. This recipe is an excellent example of how the Burmese were inspired by their neighbors to the west. It goes very well with most meat curries, Cucumber-Onion Salad (page 146), and Pepper Water (page 43).

1 1/2 cups yellow split peas
6 cups water
2 cups rice, well rinsed and drained
4 tablespoons butter
2 bay leaves
2 whole cloves
1/2 teaspoon salt
1 cup shelled fresh green peas
  (about 1 pound unshelled)

In a medium-sized saucepan, combine the split peas and the water. Bring to a boil and boil gently until half-cooked, 15 to 25 minutes. Drain the split peas.

In the same saucepan, combine the half-cooked split peas, rice, butter, bay leaves, cloves, and salt. Shake the pan to level the surface of the rice mixture. Add water slowly until it reaches 1 inch above the level of the rice mixture.

Bring the rice mixture to a boil over medium-high heat and boil for 3 minutes. Immediately reduce the heat to very low. Cover and cook for 20 minutes. Add the green peas, stir thoroughly, re-cover and cook for 3 minutes.

Serves 4.

Special celebrations in Burma call for a dish of steaming coconut rice. Or during the scorching days of summer a family will cook this rice dish when a break in the weather brings cooling breezes. Coconut milk is the main ingredient and the process of extracting the milk from the coconut is an experience in itself. First, the outer fibrous husk is removed with a razor-sharp machete. The coconut is then held in the palm of one hand and tapped repeatedly with the blunt edge of the machete until the nut breaks open. The sweet, clear juice inside the coconut is poured off into a bowl, to be used for drinking. Then, each coconut half is held onto the curved, serrated-bladed head of a steel apparatus. When the handle of the apparatus is turned, the blade shreds the meat. The shreds are put into a cloth and squeezed for their milk. Can you imagine doing all this on a very hot day? Now in America, thanks to Thai exporters, a large can of coconut milk is available for under eighty cents.

> 2 cups long-grain white rice,
>   well rinsed and drained
> 2 cups canned coconut milk
> 1 yellow onion, cut into eighths
> 1 tablespoon vegetable oil
> 1/2 teaspoon granulated sugar
> 1/2 teaspoon salt

Combine all of the ingredients in a saucepan and shake the pan to level the surface of rice mixture. Add water slowly until it reaches 1 inch above the level of the rice mixture. Stir to mix well and level the surface of the rice again.

Bring the rice to a boil over medium-high heat and immediately reduce the heat to very low. Cover and cook for 30 minutes.

Serves 4.

Thorebut Htamin
Butter Rice with Raisins and Cashew Nuts

Although this rice dish is Indian in origin, the Burmese touch—fewer spices and a subtler flavor—makes it quite different. Our family had many Indian friends for dinner and they never failed to be fascinated by the way we interpreted their cuisine. For the best result, use the Indian clarified butter called ghee. I highly recommend that you accompany the rice with mango pickle or Cauliflower Pickle (page 186).

2 cups long-grain white rice, well rinsed and drained
1 cup (1/2 pound) ghee or butter, cut into pieces
1/4 teaspoon salt
1 teaspoon salt
1/4 teaspoon ground black pepper
1 cup golden raisins
1 cup roasted cashew nuts

Combine the rice, ghee, sugar, salt, and pepper in a saucepan, mix well, and shake the pan to level the surface of the rice mixture. Add water slowly until it reaches 1 inch above the surface of the rice mixture.

Bring the rice mixture to a boil over medium-high heat and boil for 3 minutes, stirring well. Reduce the heat to very low, cover, and cook for 20 minutes.

Add the raisins and cashews and stir thoroughly to mix them evenly with the rice. Let stand, covered, for 15 minutes before serving.

Serves 4.

Htamin Kyaw
Fried Rice

Chinese fried rice is eaten at all times of the day, but the Burmese version is only eaten at breakfast. Traditionally, we add sprouted garden peas to the rice. Another breakfast favorite is the same cooked green peas with a Burmese flat bread called nanpyar. *Green garden peas take about three days to sprout, so instead I use garbanzo beans, which make an excellent substitute.*

2 eggs
1/4 teaspoon ground turmeric
1/4 cup vegetable oil
4 cups leftover cooked rice, stored in the refrigerator
1 teaspoon salt
1/4 cup finely sliced green onion
1 can (16 ounces) garbanzo beans, drained

In a bowl, break the eggs, add the turmeric, and beat lightly.

Heat the oil in a large frying pan over medium-high heat. Add the eggs and cook gently until beginning to set. Add the rice, salt, green onion, and garbanzo beans and fry over high heat for 10 minutes, stirring frequently.

Serves 4.

Kaungnyin Paung

Sweet Rice with Black-Eyed Peas

I call this rice dish the farmer's breakfast. Burmese farmers get up in the cool hours around dawn to avoid having to work under the severe heat of the midday sun. Before going out to the fields, they fill themselves up on this rice dish, which is served with dried fish and sometimes a sprinkling of salted sesame powder. It is also one of the most popular breakfast snacks enjoyed by city people. I often prepare this rice dish and fried chicken for outdoor painting trips with my American artist friends. Eating it in the countryside calls to mind happy images of Burma days.

1 1/2 cups black-eyed peas
4 1/2 cups water
2 cups glutinous rice, well rinsed and drained
Roasted Salt and Sesame Powder (following recipe)

Rinse the peas in cold water. Place the peas in a bowl, add water to cover, and let stand overnight. Drain off the soaking water and transfer the black-eyed peas to a saucepan. Add the water and bring to a boil. Boil the black-eyed peas gently until half-cooked, about 30 minutes. Drain the peas.

In the same saucepan, combine the half-cooked peas and the rice, mix well, and shake the pan to level the surface of the rice mixture. Add water slowly until it reaches 1 inch above the level of the rice mixture.

Bring the rice mixture to a boil over medium-high heat and boil for 3 minutes. Reduce the heat to very low. Cover and cook for 20 minutes, stirring every 10 minutes. Let it stand, covered, for 15 minutes before serving.

Meanwhile, prepare the Roasted Salt and Sesame Powder. Top each serving of rice with a spoonful of the sesame powder.

Serves 4.

Roasted Salt and Sesame Powder

A good condiment for rice dishes.

> 5 tablespoons sesame seed
> 1 1/2 teaspoons salt

Heat a small skillet over medium-low heat. Add the sesame seed and salt and stir constantly until the seeds are light brown, 3 to 4 minutes. Transfer the seed mixture to a blender and grind to a powder.

Makes about 1/2 cup.

For this chapter I have selected only those desserts that are commonly served at ceremonies or whipped up in the kitchen on demand. The list is rather short.

An endless variety of desserts is found in Burma's markets and at its many pagoda festivals. But these often require great effort, time, and, above all, special talent. They are not things Burmese would prepare at home. On the other hand, a wide array of tropical fresh fruits are enjoyed after every meal. Mangoes and mangosteens are particular favorites.

I remember that when I was a child my cousins and I craved mangoes during the off season. As soon as the mango season began, we begged our mothers to buy us some. We were always told to wait until the prices had come down a bit. We would sulk inconsolately. Then one day, they would bring in a large basket filled with perhaps a hundred mangoes, and we were then allowed to sit around the basket and enjoy ourselves. My mother and my aunt stood beside us holding a cane. We had to finish all the mangoes, they said, or else be spanked with the cane. It was a loving joke on their part and of course no one was ever struck. But we would have our fill and afterward no one would mention the fruit for the rest of the season.

Burma's tropical climate ensures that the country will be rich with many fruit varieties the year-round. I grew up surrounded by a garden that had mango, jackfruit, papaya, guava, custard apple, pomegranate, and tamarind trees. In 1985, driving through Port St. Lucie, Florida, I saw mango trees for the first time in thirteen years. I had to stop and sit underneath their branches for an hour to experience once again the sweet shade of Burma.

Fresh fruit is the most commonly eaten dessert in Burma. The favorites are mango, the red-husked mangosteen, and the controversial durian, a large, sharp-spiked fruit with soft pulp and a disagreeable smell. Because of the strong aroma, people either love durian or detest it. Sir James Scott, a Victorian traveler, described the experience of biting into this notorious fruit as "eating a garlic custard over a London sewer."

Although some tropical fruits can be purchased fresh at Asian markets in this country, the prices are often exorbitant. Many exotic fruits are available canned, however, and they can be quite acceptable. Look for mangosteen, jackfruit, lychee, rambutan, toddy palm seed, and longan. Durian pulp is available frozen, usually in half-pound packages. Fresh is always better, of course, but you should try the canned and frozen products for the experience.

Kyauk Kyaw
Agar-agar with Coconut

This dish is almost certain to be served at ceremonial occasions, for it is a light, pleasant taste to follow a heavy meal. It is also interesting visually, as the coconut milk rises to the top and the agar-agar settles at the bottom, forming two distinct, attractive layers. Agar-agar, a gelling agent made from seaweed, comes in three forms: powder, thin strands, and rectangular sticks.

1 packet (1.5 ounces) agar-agar in strand form
6 cups water
1 cup granulated sugar
1 tablespoon rose water
1/4 teaspoon salt
4 cups canned coconut milk

Combine the agar-agar and water in a medium-sized saucepan over medium heat. Bring to a simmer and cook, stirring continuously, until the agar-agar dissolves. Add the sugar, rose water, salt, and coconut milk. Simmer uncovered, stirring frequently, for 20 minutes.

Pour the agar-agar mixture into a 12-inch-square 3-inch-deep baking dish and let cool until set. Cover and refrigerate for at least 3 hours.

To serve, cut the mold into 2-inch-long diamond-shaped pieces.

Serves 8.

The city of Bassein, a major port in Burma's delta area, is famous for this dessert. When people visit Bassein, they always bring this dessert back as a gift. The semolina flour (called suji *by the Indians and* shwegi *by the Burmese) is available in Indian markets and some supermarkets.*

2 cups semolina flour
4 eggs, lightly beaten
4 cups canned coconut milk
^{1}/$_2$ cup milk
1 cup granulated sugar
4 cups water
^{3}/$_4$ cup vegetable oil
^{1}/$_2$ cup golden raisins
^{1}/$_2$ cup slivered blanched almonds
^{1}/$_2$ cup white poppy seed
^{1}/$_2$ pound butter, melted

Heat a dry frying pan over medium-low heat. Add the semolina flour and stir constantly until light brown, about 3 minutes. Place the flour in a mixing bowl and mix in the eggs, coconut milk, milk, sugar, and water.

Heat the oil in a medium-sized saucepan over medium heat. Add the semolina mixture and cook uncovered, stirring frequently, until the liquid evaporates and the mixture becomes pasty, about 30 minutes.

Meanwhile, preheat a broiler. Mix the raisins into the semolina and then pour the mixture into a 12-inch-square, 3-inch deep flameproof baking dish. Smooth the surface with the back of a wooden spoon. Sprinkle the almonds and poppy seed on top and then pour the melted butter evenly over the surface. Place dish in the broiler and broil until lightly browned, about 3 minutes. Transfer the dish to a preheated 250° F oven and bake until firmly set, about 15 minutes.

Remove from the oven and let cool. To serve, cut into 2-by-3-inch pieces.

Serves 8.

Agar-agar
A gelling agent made from seaweed, agar-agar is colorless and comes in three forms: powder; thin, flat strands; and rectangular sticks. It is available at most Asian markets, usually packaged in cellophane.

Bamboo shoot
Asian markets generally sell two types of bamboo shoot, canned and fresh. Canned bamboo shoots are parboiled, mild in flavor, and almost odorless. Fresh shoots, which have a more pungent aroma and flavor, are kept covered in water in large open buckets. They are not parboiled but cleaned and trimmed. The Burmese prefer the latter. Occasionally you will also see untrimmed shoots in the market.

Banana leaf
In Burma banana leaves are abundant and free for the taking, much as ice is for the Eskimos. The Burmese would shake their heads and laugh in disgust that in America the leaves are actually sold for money. Banana leaves are available frozen at most Mexican and Southeast Asian food markets. Each plastic package usually contains six 1-foot square pieces.

Bean curd sheets
Very dry and brittle before soaking, these pale yellow sheets have a shiny surface that gives them a distinctive look. They come in 17-ounce plastic-wrapped packets. Not a single Chinese market is without them.

Bean thread noodles
Cook these noodles and you'll see why they are also known as silver noodles, cellophane noodles, and glass noodles. Made from mung bean starch, they look like fishing line when raw. Bean thread noodles are most commonly sold in a large package that contains six 1.75-ounce individual packets.

Bitter melon
Although bitter melon (also known as bitter gourd) looks and is shaped like a cucumber, its crude surface may have given it a complex, causing it to become bitter. When cooked with onions and tomatoes, the bitter taste is tamed and brought into harmony. The Burmese, the Chinese, and the Indian consider bitter melon a delight maybe because bitterness is part of life.

Black fungus
Also known in English as wood ears, black fungus is called *Ahpogyinaywet*, which means "old man's ears," in Burma. Burmese men tend to sprout hair on their ears when they reach about sixty; from afar these old men look as if they have black ears. Always soak the fungus in water for about 30 minutes before cooking; you'll

notice that the size increases threefold during this step. Black fungus has no definite taste, but adds texture and color to a dish. Look for it in 4-ounce plastic packets.

Black mustard seed

This tiny seed has an olivelike nutty taste. The way to taste one is, with the help of your tongue, to place a seed carefully between the front teeth and then crack it open gently. Never chew a spoonful of the seeds as you would caviar. They must be boiled, roasted, or sautéed before eating. They add a subtle flavor, to dishes and enhance them visually. Black mustard seeds are available in Indian shops, usually sold in bulk or in small cellophane packets.

Bottleneck gourd

This pale green squash, with a slender neck and wide body, has been known to grow as large as 4 feet long and 1 foot in diameter in Burma. The larger gourds are dried to use as vessels and utensils. The smaller, younger gourds are best for cooking.

Broad beans, fried

Also known as fava beans and horse beans, crisply fried broad beans make a great snack. Packaged in airtight bags, the beans can be found in Chinese and Vietnamese food markets.

Cardamom

Harvested from a plant belonging to the ginger family, tiny, black, aromatic cardamom seeds are used whole, ground, and even sometimes while still in their white husks in cooking. They are believed to aid digestion. Look for cardamom in Asian markets and supermarkets.

Chana dal powder

Chana dal looks very much like yellow split peas, except a bit smaller. Chana dal powder is called *paemoht* in Burmese and *besan* in Hindi. The Burmese use the powder as a thickener in soups and toast it for seasoning salads. It can be easily found at Indian food markets and keeps well in a closed jar at room temperature.

Chicken stock

The best chicken stock is homemade and it is rather simple to make. All you need to do to make a Burmese-style stock is to skin a whole chicken and then simmer it in 10 cups water with 3 slices fresh ginger, 4 whole black peppercorns, 1 tablespoon salt, and 1 yellow onion, sliced, for about 1 hour. Canned stock is fine if you are short of time.

Cilantro, fresh

Also known as Chinese parsley, cilantro is the Spanish name for fresh coriander. The fragrant, flat-leaf herb is a favorite of Southeast Asian cooks.

Coconut milk

Coconut milk comes from squeezing freshly grated coconut through a cotton cloth. In the United States nobody in their right mind makes their own coconut milk. The convenience, quality, and low cost of canned coconut milk imported from Thailand makes preparing it fresh impractical. Coconut milk is usually sold in cans that hold about 16 ounces; do not buy the sweetened coconut milk used for making tropical drinks.

Coriander seed

Coriander seeds come from an aromatic plant that belongs to the carrot family. Their scent is a combination of citrus and onions. They are an important spice, either whole or ground, in curries and pickles.

Curry leaves

Known in India as *kari patta*, curry leaves are a sweeter, milder version of bay leaves. On occasion you'll find fresh curry leaves at Indian stores; most often, however, you will have to settle for dried ones.

Daikon

In Japanese the word *daikon* means "great root" This long, white radish, with a crisp texture and fresh taste, has a smooth, tight skin when fresh and can be found in many American supermarkets. It is eaten raw or cooked and is said to help in the digestion of oily foods.

Dried lily flowers

These long, thin buds of the lily flower are also called golden needles or tiger-lily petals. They must be soaked in cold water to cover for about 30 minutes so that their bitter pale yellow pollen doesn't interfere with the flavor of the dish. Tie each bud in a knot to keep them from breaking during cooking. They are sold at all Asian food markets in cellophane bags.

Extra-thin noodles

When compared to these noodles, bean thread noodles look overweight. These hairline strands are about $1/64$ inch thick, making them the thinnest of all thin noodles. They are made of wheat flour and come in packages that consist of six bunches delicately folded. Look for them at most Chinese markets.

Fenugreek

Fenugreek, a member of the lentil family, is known as *penatha* in Burmese, which means "lentils of pleasant fragrance." Fenugreek seeds are tiny and rock hard and have a lemony aroma. They are ground to a powder for use in cooking, where only a small amount is added. Indians believe that fenugreek alleviates diabetes and fevers. Ground fenugreek keeps well in a closed jar. Look for it in Indian markets and some supermarkets.

Fish sauce

This extract of anchovy is a requisite for the Burmese tongue, and is widely used throughout Southeast Asia. It is sold in bottles, mostly imported from Thailand, and can easily be found at any Southeast Asian food market.

Ghee

To be more precise, this entry should be called *usli ghee*. In the West, ghee is commonly referred to as clarified butter, but making *usli ghee* is more involved than simply melting butter and decanting the clear liquid from the milk solids as the French do. First, in a large saucepan, melt 1 pound unsalted butter over very low heat; this should take about 15 minutes. Increase the heat to medium. White foam will begin to form on the surface and the butter will start to crackle. This indicates that the moisture is beginning to leave the milk solids. Cook for 10 minutes without stirring. When the moisture is completely gone, the crackling will stop and the foam will subside. Using a wooden spatula, stir the liquid constantly until the butter solids begin to brown. Immediately turn off the heat and let the brown residue settle to the bottom. When the melted butter is cool, pour the clear liquid into a jar through a double layer of cheesecloth. One pound unsalted butter will yield 1 1/2 cups of *usli ghee*. Ghee will keep in a well-sealed jar for about 2 months at room temperature and 5 months in the refrigerator.

Ginger juice

To make ginger juice, peel the skin from 6 ounces of fresh ginger and chop the pulp in a blender with 1/4 cup water. Wrap the resulting mass in cheesecloth and squeeze to extract as much juice as possible. It should yield 2 tablespoons or more of juice.

Ginger root

This light brown, knobby root comes from a bamboolike tropical plant. Piquant in flavor and of pungent aroma, fresh ginger is available in the produce section of many supermarkets. Dried ginger slices and ground ginger should not be substituted for fresh. Store ginger in a covered jar in the refrigerator.

Glutinous rice

Also known as sticky rice or sweet rice, glutinous rice is short-grained and is whiter than other common rice varieties and has a silver shine to its surface. It indeed becomes sticky when cooked, but it is not sweet. The name "sweet" comes from its being used in the making of desserts. The Burmese eat this rice for breakfast and long-grained white rice for lunch and dinner. Store it in a plastic bag or jar in a dry, cool place.

Glutinous rice flour

This flour is made by grinding glutinous rice kernels to a fine powder. It is used in the making of sweets, batters for frying, and as an thickener. Look for this flour in 1-pound bags or boxes in any Asian food market. It keeps well in a tightly closed jar.

Lemongrass

At first glance, the lemongrass plant looks like an iris plant. The lemony fragrance that gives it its distinctive quality lies in the bulb, or head, that is buried beneath the ground's surface. The fresh bulb is crushed so that the scent is released to infuse fully simmering soups or curries. Lemongrass is widely used in Southeast Asian cuisines for its aromatic property. Ground dried lemongrass, available in jars and cellophane packages, is used for marinades. Both the fresh and ground varieties are available at Asian food markets. Buy only the amount of fresh lemongrass you need, as it does not keep well.

Long beans

Also known as Chinese green beans, long beans look like the common string bean, but they grow to 2 feet in length. They are usually sold in 2-pound bundles tied at the stems; remove the stems before cooking. Long beans are generally cut into 2-inch lengths for stir-frying or they can be simply cooked briefly in boiling water. Long beans keep up to 3 days in a plastic bag in the refrigerator.

Mung beans

Mung beans come from the pod of the mung bean plant. There are two types available at Asian markets: dried whole mung beans with dark green husks, and dried yellow split mung beans, which have the husks removed. The Burmese prefer the latter. Mung beans keep well in a tightly closed jar in a cool, dry place.

Mustard greens, preserved

Broad-leaved, dark green Chinese mustard, which is also known as mustard cabbage, is preserved in brine and then packed in 16-ounce air-tight plastic packets. Rinse the brine off thoroughly before cooking. The greens are available at Chinese markets; buy only as much as you need.

Poppy seed

These seeds come from poppies and definitely won't make you high. They are either dark purple, the most commonly used type in the West, or white. The Burmese use the white seeds to give a crunchy crust to desserts. Buy only what you need and store in a tightly closed jar.

Rice flour

This flour is simply white rice kernels that have been ground to a powder. Rice flour is used in batters for frying, pastries, as a thickener, and for making rice stick and other rice noodles. Sold in 1-pound air-tight plastic bags at Asian groceries, keeps well in a tightly closed jar.

Sesame oil, Asian

Sesame oil is made from grinding hot, roasted sesame seeds and squeezing the grounds for oil. This type of sesame oil has the color of a good Cognac and is an integral part of Asian cooking. Do not confuse Asian sesame oil with the much clearer version found in supermarkets and health-food stores. It is sold in 8-ounce bottles at Asian food markets. Store the oil in the refrigerator.

Shrimp, dried

These are shrimp that have been shelled and dried in the sun. They are priced according to size. Large-sized dried shrimp sometimes sell for as high as $20 per pound. Dried shrimp are used as a flavoring, are eaten as a snack, or are barbecued. Store them in a well-sealed jar in the refrigerator. They will keep for months.

Shrimp powder

The use of the word *powder* is misleading. Actually shrimp powder is dried shrimp that has been shredded into very fine flakes. You can buy it already shredded or shred your own dried shrimp in a blender. Excellent for flavoring soups and salads, shrimp powder is widely used throughout Southeast Asia.

Soy sauce, light and dark

Soy sauce is an extraction of boiled, fermented, salted soybeans. Although there are grades in between, light and dark soy sauces are the most commonly used. Light soy sauce is thin and is used as a table condiment and in cooking delicately flavored dishes. Dark soy sauce is much thicker in consistency and contains molasses. Soy sauces keep well in a tightly closed bottle at room temperature.

Sriracha chile sauce

Sriracha chile sauce is a mixture of red chile, salt, garlic, sugar, and vinegar. A distinctive bright red-orange color, it has the consistency of ketchup. Sriracha sauce is made in Thailand and most often comes in 24-ounce bottles. Store it at room temperature.

Tamarind juice

Tamarind is the fruit, or pod, of the tamarind tree. It has a sour taste and is widely used as a seasoning in Asia and in Central America. The pods are left on the tree to dry in the sun before they are picked and stored. Sold in pods, slabs, or paste form at Asian and Latin American food markets, tamarind will keep for up to a year if refrigerated. The pods are the best form to use, while the paste is the least desirable. To make tamarind juice, soak four 3-inch-long pods or a 2-by-2-inch slab in 3/4 cup warm water for 30 minutes then mash well using your fingers.

Pour the mixture through a fine-mesh strainer to remove the seeds and pulp. This amount should yield about 1/4 cup juice.

Turmeric

Turmeric is a root that is closely related to ginger. The root is dried and ground to a powder and then used in small amounts. It gives many curries their traditional bright yellow hue, which signifies gold. It is also used as a fabric dye. The Burmese strongly believe that turmeric has healing power. Most Burmese meat dishes call for marinating the meat with turmeric as a protection against germs and bacteria. Readily available at Indian food stores and in supermarket spice sections, turmeric will keep indefinitely in a tightly closed jar.

Water spinach

Also called swamp cabbage and *ong choy* and *tung choy* in Chinese, water spinach is a hollow-stemmed plant with dark green leaves that look like the heads of spears. Except for the tough lower part of the stem, the whole plant is edible. It is excellent is stir-fries and soups and is sold by the bunch at Asian food markets, usually in spring and early summer.

Wheat flour noodles

Commonly sold by their Japanese name, *somen*, these fine, white noodles are made from hard wheat. *Somen* comes in different forms. The threadlike variety is similar to the type of noodle the Burmese use for their famous fish soup, *mohingar*. In Burma *mohingar* noodles are made from slightly fermented rice flour. But in America we have to settle for Tomoshigara brand *somen*, which is available at Asian food markets.

Worcestershire sauce

The British ruled Burma for 63 years, until 1948. During the colonial period, many Burmese cooks were trained by the British. For this reason, the Burmese came to use very small amounts of Worcestershire sauce in some of their dishes. Lea and Perrins is the preferred brand in Burma, just as it is in the West.

Yellow split pea

Dried yellow garden peas that have been husked and split are called yellow split peas or, in India, *vatana*. Chana dal, which is a different split pea, can be substituted, as it is very similar. Store the peas in a tightly closed jar in a dry, cool place. Yellow split peas are also sold fried in cellophane packets labeled "chana fried."